Fun Stuff With

HERSHEY'S®

Publications International, Ltd.

Pictured on the front cover *(clockwise from top right)*: White Chip and Macadamia Toffee Crunch *(page 46)*, Peanut Butter Blossoms *(page 28)*, Ice Cream Sandwiches *(page 4)*, and HERSHEY'S® KISSES® Mice *(page 117)*.
Pictured on the inside front flap: HERSHEY'S® KISSES® Birthday Cake *(page 27)*.
Pictured on the back cover *(left to right)*: Mini Chocolate Pies *(page 62)*, Two Great Tastes Pudding Parfaits *(page 71)* and Peanut Butter and Milk Chocolate Chip Cattails *(page 36)*.
Pictured on the inside back flap: Dutch Country Dirt *(page 34)*

ISBN-13: 978-1-4508-7040-5
ISBN-10: 1-4508-7040-6

Library of Congress Control Number: 2013932211

Manufactured in China.

06/22/2013 Guangdong

136471HF4

8 7 6 5 4 3 2 1

Microwave Cooking: Microwave ovens vary in wattage. Use the cooking times as guidelines and check for doneness before adding more time.

table of Contents

just for Kids

Ice Cream Sandwiches

makes about 12 (4-inch) ice cream sandwiches

½ cup shortening

1 cup sugar

1 egg

1 teaspoon vanilla extract

1⅔ cups all-purpose flour

⅓ cup HERSHEY'S Cocoa

½ teaspoon baking soda

½ teaspoon salt

¼ cup milk

Desired flavor ice cream, slightly softened

Assorted chopped HERSHEY'S, REESE'S or HEATH baking pieces, crushed peppermints or other small candies (optional)

1. Beat shortening, sugar, egg and vanilla in large bowl until well blended. Stir together flour, cocoa, baking soda and salt; add alternately with milk to sugar mixture, beating until well blended. Cover; refrigerate about 1 hour.

2. Heat oven to 375°F. Drop batter by heaping tablespoons onto ungreased cookie sheet. With palm of hand or bottom of glass, flatten each cookie into 2¾-inch circle, about ¼ inch thick. Bake 8 to 10 minutes or until almost set. Cool 1 minute; remove from cookie sheet to wire rack. Cool completely.

3. Place scoop of ice cream on flat side of 1 cookie; spread evenly with spatula. Top with another cookie, pressing together lightly; repeat with remaining cookies. Roll ice cream edges in chopped baking pieces or candies, if desired. Wrap individually in foil; freeze until firm.

HUGS® & KISSES® Crescents

makes 8 crescents

1 **package (8 ounces) refrigerated crescent dinner rolls**

24 **HERSHEY'S KISSES**BRAND **Milk Chocolates or HERSHEY'S HUGS**BRAND **Candies**

Powdered sugar

1. Heat oven to 375°F. Separate dough into 8 triangles. Remove wrappers from chocolates.

2. Place 2 chocolates at center of wide end of each triangle; place an additional chocolate on top of other two pieces. Starting at wide end, roll to opposite point; pinch edges to seal. Place rolls, pointed side down, on ungreased cookie sheet. Curve into crescent shape.

3. Bake 10 minutes or until lightly browned. Cool slightly; sift with powdered sugar. Serve warm.

Note: Leftover crescents can be reheated in microwave for a few seconds.

Meltaway Brownie Bites

makes about 48 brownie bites

48   Any flavor **HERSHEY'S KISSES**BRAND **Chocolates** or **HERSHEY'S HUGS**BRAND **Candies**

⅔   **cup butter or margarine, softened**

1¼   **cups granulated sugar**

1   **tablespoon water**

1   **teaspoon vanilla extract**

2   **eggs**

1½   **cups all-purpose flour**

½   **cup HERSHEY'S Cocoa** or **HERSHEY'S SPECIAL DARK Cocoa**

½   **teaspoon salt**

¼   **teaspoon baking soda**

     Powdered sugar

1. Remove wrappers from chocolates; place in freezer while preparing and baking cookies.

2. Beat butter, granulated sugar, water and vanilla in large bowl on medium speed of mixer until well blended. Add eggs; beat well. Stir together flour, cocoa, salt and baking soda. Gradually add to sugar mixture, beating on low speed until blended. Cover; refrigerate dough about 2 hours or until firm enough to handle.

3. Heat oven to 350°F. Line 48 small muffin cups (1¾ inches in diameter) with paper or foil baking cups or lightly spray with vegetable cooking spray. Shape dough into 1-inch balls; place in prepared muffin cups.

4. Bake 11 to 13 minutes or until cookie surface is set. Cookies will appear soft and moist. Do not overbake. Cool about 5 minutes on wire rack. Dust cookie tops with powdered sugar. Press frozen chocolate piece into surface of each cookie. Cool completely in pan on wire rack.

REESE'S® Peanut Butter Temptations

makes about 42 cookies

About 40 REESE'S Peanut Butter Cups Miniatures or 12 (0.8 ounces each) REESE'S Peanut Butter Cups, quartered

½   **cup (1 stick) butter or margarine, softened**

½   **cup granulated sugar**

½   **cup packed light brown sugar**

½   **cup REESE'S Creamy Peanut Butter**

1   **egg**

½   **teaspoon vanilla extract**

1½   **cups all-purpose flour**

¾   **teaspoon baking soda**

½   **teaspoon salt**

1. Heat oven to 375°F. Remove wrappers from candies. Line small muffin cups (1¾ inches in diameter) with paper or foil bake cups, if desired.

2. Beat butter, granulated sugar, brown sugar, peanut butter, egg and vanilla until fluffy in large bowl. Stir together flour, baking soda and salt; gradually add to butter mixture, beating until well blended. Shape dough into 1-inch balls; place one in each paper-lined or ungreased muffin cup. Do not flatten.

3. Bake 10 to 12 minutes until puffed and lightly browned; remove from oven. Immediately press peanut butter cup in center of each cookie. Cool completely in muffin pan.

just for kids

Black-Eyed Susan Cheesecakes

makes about 2 dozen

24	vanilla wafer cookies
2	packages (8 ounces each) cream cheese, softened
½	cup sugar
2	eggs
½	teaspoon vanilla extract
1	cup REESE'S Peanut Butter Chips
½	cup HERSHEY'S SPECIAL DARK Chocolate Chips or HERSHEY'S Semi-Sweet Chocolate Chips
3	tablespoons butter
	Sliced almonds

1. Heat oven to 350°F. Line muffin cups with foil bake cups (2 inches in diameter*). Place one vanilla wafer, flat-side down, in bottom of each cup.

2. Beat cream cheese and sugar on medium speed of mixer in large bowl. Add eggs and vanilla; beat well. Stir in peanut butter chips. Spoon heaping tablespoon cream cheese mixture into each muffin cup.

3. Bake 15 minutes or just until set, but not browned. Cool.

4. Place chocolate chips and butter in small microwave-safe bowl. Microwave at MEDIUM (50%) 30 seconds; stir. If necessary, microwave at MEDIUM an additional 10 seconds at a time, stirring after each heating, just until chips are melted and mixture is smooth when stirred.

5. Drop about 1 teaspoon of chocolate mixture onto center of each cheesecake, letting white show around edge. Place almond slices around chocolate mixture to resemble petals. Refrigerate. Cover; refrigerate leftover cheesecakes.

*Cheesecakes may also be baked in 2½-inch foil bake cups. Divide cheesecake mixture evenly into 18 cups. Bake 20 minutes or just until set, but not browned.

just for kids

Chippy Chewy Bars

makes about 48 bars

½ cup (1 stick) butter or margarine

1½ cups graham cracker crumbs

1⅔ cups (10-ounce package) REESE'S Peanut Butter Chips

1½ cups MOUNDS Sweetened Coconut Flakes

1 can (14 ounces) sweetened condensed milk (not evaporated milk)

½ cup HERSHEY'S SPECIAL DARK Chocolate Chips, HERSHEY'S Semi-Sweet Chocolate Chips or HERSHEY'S Mini Chips Semi-Sweet Chocolate

¾ teaspoon shortening (do not use butter, margarine, spread or oil)

1. Heat oven to 350°F. Place butter in 13×9×2-inch baking pan. Heat in oven until melted; remove pan from oven. Sprinkle graham cracker crumbs evenly over butter; press down with fork.

2. Sprinkle peanut butter chips over crumbs; sprinkle coconut over chips. Drizzle sweetened condensed milk evenly over top.

3. Bake 20 minutes or until lightly browned.

4. Place chocolate chips and shortening in small microwave-safe bowl. Microwave at MEDIUM (50%) 30 seconds; stir. If necessary, microwave at MEDIUM an additional 10 seconds at a time, stirring after each heating, just until chips are melted when stirred. Drizzle evenly over top of baked mixture. Cool completely. Cut into bars.

just for kids

Rich Cocoa Crinkle Cookies

makes about 6 dozen cookies

2	cups granulated sugar
¾	cup vegetable oil
1	cup HERSHEY'S Cocoa
4	eggs
2	teaspoons vanilla extract
2⅓	cups all-purpose flour
2	teaspoons baking powder
½	teaspoon salt
	Powdered sugar

1. Combine granulated sugar and oil in large bowl; add cocoa, beating until well blended. Beat in eggs and vanilla. Stir together flour, baking powder and salt in separate bowl. Gradually add to cocoa mixture, beating well.

2. Cover; refrigerate until dough is firm enough to handle, at least 6 hours.

3. Heat oven to 350°F. Grease cookie sheet or line with parchment paper. Shape dough into 1-inch balls; roll in powdered sugar to coat. Place about 2 inches apart on prepared cookie sheet.

4. Bake 10 to 12 minutes or until almost no indentation remains when touched lightly and tops are crackled. Cool slightly. Remove from cookie sheet to wire rack. Cool completely.

1st Birthday Cupcakes

makes about 2½ dozen cupcakes

1⅔   cups all-purpose flour
1½   cups sugar
½   cup HERSHEY'S Cocoa
1½   teaspoons baking soda
1   teaspoon salt
½   teaspoon baking powder
2   eggs
½   cup shortening
1½   cups buttermilk or sour milk*
1   teaspoon vanilla extract
      ONE-BOWL BUTTERCREAM
      FROSTING (recipe follows)

*To sour milk: Use 4½ teaspoons white vinegar plus milk to equal 1½ cups.

1. Heat oven to 350°F. Line muffin cups (2½ inches in diameter) with paper bake cups.

2. Stir together flour, sugar, cocoa, baking soda, salt and baking powder in large bowl. Add eggs, shortening, buttermilk and vanilla. Beat on low speed of mixer 1 minute, scraping bowl constantly. Beat on high speed 3 minutes, scraping bowl occasionally. Fill muffin cups ½ full with batter.

3. Bake 18 to 20 minutes or until wooden pick inserted in center comes out clean. Remove from pan to wire rack. Cool completely. Frost with ONE-BOWL BUTTERCREAM FROSTING.

HERSHEY'S Chocolate Cake Variation:

Heat oven to 350°F. Grease two 9-inch round baking pans; line bottoms with wax paper. Prepare batter as directed above; pour into prepared pans. Bake 30 to 35 minutes or until wooden pick inserted in center comes out clean. Cool 10 minutes; remove from pans to wire racks. Remove paper. Cool completely. Frost with ONE-BOWL BUTTERCREAM FROSTING.

One-Bowl Buttercream Frosting

6   tablespoons butter or margarine, softened
2⅔   cups powdered sugar
½   cup HERSHEY'S Cocoa
⅓   cup milk
1   teaspoon vanilla extract

Beat butter in medium bowl. Add powdered sugar and cocoa alternately with milk and vanilla, beating to spreading consistency (additional milk may be needed).

MAKES ABOUT 2 CUPS FROSTING

just for kids

Tiny MINI KISSES® Peanut Butter Blossoms

makes about 14 dozen cookies

¾   **cup REESE'S Creamy Peanut Butter**
½   **cup shortening**
⅓   **cup granulated sugar**
⅓   **cup packed light brown sugar**
1   **egg**
3   **tablespoons milk**
1   **teaspoon vanilla extract**
1½   **cups all-purpose flour**
½   **teaspoon baking soda**
½   **teaspoon salt**
     Additional granulated sugar
     HERSHEY'S MINI KISSESBRAND
       Milk Chocolates

1. Heat oven to 350°F.

2. Beat peanut butter and shortening in large bowl with mixer until well blended. Add ⅓ cup granulated sugar and brown sugar; beat well. Add egg, milk and vanilla; beat until fluffy. Stir together flour, baking soda and salt; gradually add to peanut butter mixture, beating until blended. Shape into ½-inch balls. Roll in granulated sugar; place on ungreased cookie sheet.

3. Bake 5 to 6 minutes or until set. Immediately press chocolate into center of each cookie. Remove from cookie sheet to wire rack. Cool completely.

Variation: For larger cookies, shape dough into 1-inch balls. Roll in granulated sugar. Place on ungreased cookie sheet. Bake 10 minutes or until set. Immediately place 3 chocolate pieces in center of each cookie, pressing down slightly. Remove from cookie sheet to wire rack. Cool completely.

just for kids

Peanut Butter Cup Pinwheels

makes about 36 cookies

1	package (8 ounces) cream cheese, softened
1	cup (2 sticks) butter or margarine, softened
¼	cup granulated sugar
1	teaspoon vanilla extract
2¼	cups all-purpose flour
⅛	teaspoon salt
36	to 40 REESE'S Peanut Butter Cups Miniatures
	Additional granulated sugar
	Powdered sugar
3	tablespoons REESE'S Creamy Peanut Butter

1. Beat cream cheese, butter, ¼ cup granulated sugar and vanilla in large mixer bowl until light and fluffy. Stir together flour and salt; gradually beat into cream cheese mixture, beating until well blended. Divide dough into half; cover and refrigerate about an hour or until firm.

2. Remove wrappers from peanut butter cups. Carefully place each peanut butter cup on its side and cut through the cup, separating the top from the peanut butter filling and bottom. Set the peanut butter cup tops aside. Chop the bottom sections with a little bit of granulated sugar into very fine pieces; set aside. (The granulated sugar helps to keep the mixture from clumping.)

3. Heat oven to 350°F. Line cookie sheets with parchment paper or grease lightly. Roll half of dough at a time on lightly floured surface to a thickness of ⅛ inch. (Keep remaining dough in refrigerator until ready to use.) Cut into 3-inch squares. Use spatula to lift and place squares 1 inch apart on prepared cookie sheets.

4. Place about 1 teaspoon of chopped peanut butter cup mixture in center of each square. Cut from each corner of square to within ½ inch of center and filling. Bring every other point into center and press dough together to form pinwheel.

5. Bake 12 to 14 minutes or until lightly browned. Cool cookies completely. Sprinkle cookies with powdered sugar. "Glue" peanut butter cup top to cookie with about ¼ teaspoon peanut butter to form center of pinwheel.

Chocolate Swirl Lollipop Cookies

makes about 24 cookies

½	cup (1 stick) butter or margarine, softened
1	cup sugar
2	eggs
1	teaspoon orange extract
1	teaspoon vanilla extract
2¼	cups all-purpose flour, divided
½	teaspoon baking soda
½	teaspoon salt
¼	teaspoon freshly grated orange peel
	Few drops red and yellow food color (optional)
2	sections (½ ounce each) HERSHEY'S Unsweetened Chocolate Baking Bar
	About 24 wooden ice cream sticks

1. Beat butter and sugar in large bowl until blended. Add eggs and extracts; beat until light and fluffy. Gradually add 1¼ cups flour, blending until smooth. Stir in remaining 1 cup flour, baking soda and salt until mixture is well blended.

2. Place half of batter in medium bowl; stir in orange peel. Stir in food color, if desired. Melt chocolate as directed on package; stir into remaining half of batter. Cover; refrigerate both mixtures until firm enough to roll.

3. With rolling pin or fingers, between 2 pieces of wax paper, roll chocolate and orange mixtures each into 10×8-inch rectangle. Remove wax paper; place orange mixture on top of chocolate. Starting on longest side, roll up doughs tightly, forming into 12-inch roll; wrap in plastic wrap. Refrigerate until firm.

4. Heat oven to 350°F. Remove plastic wrap from roll; cut into ½-inch-wide slices. Place on cookie sheet at least 3 inches apart. Insert popsicle stick into each cookie.

5. Bake 8 to 10 minutes or until cookie is almost set. Cool slightly; remove from cookie sheet to wire rack. Cool completely. Decorate and tie with ribbon, if desired.

Pears in Paradise

makes 1 serving

2 tablespoons HERSHEY'S Syrup

½ cup vanilla ice cream

1 to 2 tablespoons HERSHEY'S Caramel Topping

1 pear half, canned

½ teaspoon cinnamon-sugar

⅓ cup additional HERSHEY'S Syrup
   Whipped cream

2 teaspoons toasted pecan pieces*

To toast pecans: Heat oven to 350°F. Place pecans in single layer in shallow baking pan. Bake 7 to 8 minutes, stirring occasionally, until light brown. Cool completely.

1. Pour 2 tablespoons chocolate syrup into bottom of chilled bowl or stemmed dessert glass. Top with ice cream; drizzle with caramel topping.

2. Place pear half on caramel; sprinkle with cinnamon-sugar. Drizzle with additional ⅓ cup chocolate syrup. Garnish with whipped cream rosettes and toasted pecans.

KISSed Pretzel S'mores

make as desired

Small pretzels (twisted)
Miniature marshmallows
HERSHEY'S KISSESBRAND **Milk Chocolates**

1. Heat oven to 350°F. Line cookie sheet with parchment paper or foil.

2. Place 1 pretzel for each pretzel s'more desired on prepared sheet. Top each pretzel with 3 marshmallows and another pretzel.

3. Bake 4 to 5 minutes or until marshmallows soften and begin to puff. Remove from oven and gently press chocolate on each top pretzel. Allow treats to sit several minutes in order for chocolate pieces to melt enough to adhere to pretzels and to soften slightly. Treats are best if eaten while chocolate piece is soft.

Brownie Cupcakes

makes 18 cupcakes

1	cup (2 sticks) butter or margarine
½	cup HERSHEY'S Cocoa
1	cup packed light brown sugar
½	cup granulated sugar
3	eggs
1	teaspoon vanilla extract
1	cup all-purpose flour
1⅓	cups chopped nuts, divided

1. Heat oven to 350°F. Line 2½-inch muffin cups with paper or foil bake cups.

2. Place butter in large microwave-safe bowl. Microwave at HIGH (100%) 1½ minutes or until melted. Add cocoa; stir until smooth.

Add brown sugar and granulated sugar; stir with spoon until well blended. Add eggs and vanilla; beat well with spoon. Add flour and 1 cup nuts; stir until well blended.

3. Fill prepared muffin cups about ⅔ full with batter. Sprinkle about 1 teaspoon remaining nuts over top of each.

4. Bake 22 to 25 minutes or until tops are cracked and feel firm (will be moist inside). Cool in cups on wire rack about 15 minutes. Remove from cups. Cool completely.

family faves

Whoopie Pie Cookies

makes about 36 filled cookies

½	cup shortening
1	cup sugar
1	egg
1	teaspoon vanilla extract
1¾	cups all-purpose flour
½	cup HERSHEY'S Cocoa
1¼	teaspoons baking soda
⅛	teaspoon salt
1	cup buttermilk or sour milk*

CREME FILLING (recipe follows)

To sour milk: Use 1 tablespoon white vinegar plus milk to equal 1 cup.

1. Heat oven to 375°F. Lightly grease cookie sheet or line with parchment paper.

2. Beat shortening and sugar in large bowl until well blended. Add egg and vanilla; beat well. Stir together flour, cocoa, baking soda and salt; add alternately with buttermilk to shortening mixture. Drop by teaspoons onto prepared cookie sheet.

3. Bake 7 to 8 minutes or until cookies spring back when touched lightly in center. Remove from cookie sheet to wire rack. Cool completely. Prepare CREME FILLING. Place 2 cookies, flat sides together, with about 1 tablespoon filling.

Creme Filling

¼	cup (½ stick) butter or margarine, softened
¼	cup shortening
1	cup marshmallow creme
1¼	cups powdered sugar
1½	teaspoons vanilla extract
¼	cup chopped maraschino cherries, well drained (optional)

1. Beat butter and shortening in medium bowl until creamy. Gradually add marshmallow creme, beating well.

2. Gradually add powdered sugar and vanilla, beating until well blended. Stir in cherries, if desired.

MAKES ABOUT 1½ CUPS FILLING

Mini Cocoa Cupcake Kabobs

makes about 4 dozen cupcakes

1	cup sugar
1	cup all-purpose flour
⅓	cup HERSHEY'S Cocoa
¾	teaspoon baking powder
¾	teaspoon baking soda
½	teaspoon salt
1	egg
½	cup milk
¼	cup vegetable oil
1	teaspoon vanilla extract
½	cup boiling water
	LICKETY-SPLIT COCOA FROSTING (recipe follows)
	Jelly beans or sugar nonpareils and/or decorating frosting
	Marshmallows
	Strawberries
	Wooden or metal skewers

1. Heat oven to 350°F. Spray small muffin cups (1¾ inches in diameter) with vegetable cooking spray.

2. Stir together sugar, flour, cocoa, baking powder, baking soda and salt in medium bowl. Add egg, milk, oil and vanilla; beat on medium speed of mixer 2 minutes. Stir in boiling water (batter will be thin). Fill muffin cups about ⅔ full with batter.

3. Bake 10 minutes or until wooden pick inserted in center comes out clean. Cool slightly; remove from pans to wire racks. Cool completely. Frost with LICKETY-SPLIT COCOA FROSTING. Garnish with jelly beans, nonpareils and/or frosting piped onto cupcake. Alternate cupcakes, marshmallows and strawberries on skewers.

Lickety-Split Cocoa Frosting: Beat 3 tablespoons softened butter or margarine in small bowl until creamy. Add 1¼ cups powdered sugar, ¼ cup HERSHEY'S Cocoa, 2 to 3 tablespoons milk and ½ teaspoon vanilla extract until smooth and of desired consistency. Makes about 1 cup frosting.

Note: Number of kabobs will be determined by length of skewer used and number of cupcakes, marshmallows and strawberries placed on each skewer.

family faves

Chocolate Dessert Waffles

makes about 10 (4-inch) waffles

½   cup HERSHEY'S Cocoa
¼   cup (½ stick) butter or margarine, melted
¾   cup sugar
2   eggs
2   teaspoons vanilla extract
1   cup all-purpose flour
½   teaspoon baking soda
½   teaspoon salt
½   cup buttermilk or sour milk*
½   cup chopped nuts (optional)
    HOT FUDGE SAUCE (recipe follows)
    STRAWBERRY DESSERT CREAM or APPLE-CINNAMON TOPPING or PEACH-NUTMEG TOPPING or CHOCOLATE MAPLE SAUCE (recipes follow)

*To sour milk: Use 1½ teaspoons white vinegar plus milk to equal ½ cup.

1. Stir cocoa and butter in large bowl until smooth; stir in sugar. Add eggs and vanilla; beat well. Stir together flour, baking soda and salt; add alternately with buttermilk to cocoa mixture. Stir in nuts, if desired.

2. Bake in waffle iron according to manufacturer's directions. Carefully remove waffle from iron. Serve with desired toppings.

Note: Leftover waffles may be frozen; thaw in toaster on low heat.

Hot Fudge Sauce

¾   cup sugar
½   cup HERSHEY'S Cocoa
½   cup plus 2 tablespoons (5-ounce can) evaporated milk
⅓   cup light corn syrup
⅓   cup butter or margarine
1   teaspoon vanilla extract

Combine sugar and cocoa in small saucepan; stir in evaporated milk and corn syrup. Cook over medium heat, stirring constantly, until mixture boils; boil and stir 1 minute. Remove from heat. Add butter and vanilla; stirring until butter is melted. Serve warm.

MAKES ABOUT 1¾ CUPS SAUCE

Strawberry Dessert Cream: Beat 1 cup (½ pint) cold whipping cream in small bowl until stiff. Fold in ⅓ cup strawberry preserves and 3 drops red food color, if desired. Makes about 2 cups topping.

Apple-Cinnamon Topping: Heat 1 can (21 ounces) apple pie filling, 1 tablespoon butter or margarine and ⅛ teaspoon ground cinnamon in small saucepan until warm.

Peach-Nutmeg Topping: Heat 1 can (21 ounces) peach pie filling and ⅛ teaspoon ground nutmeg in small saucepan until warm.

family faves

Chocolate Maple Sauce

¾ cup sugar

⅓ cup HERSHEY'S Cocoa

¾ cup evaporated milk

¼ cup (½ stick) butter or margarine

⅛ teaspoon salt

½ teaspoon maple flavor

½ teaspoon vanilla extract

Combine sugar and cocoa in small saucepan; stir in evaporated milk. Cook over medium heat, stirring constantly, until mixture boils; boil and stir 1 minute. Remove from heat. Add butter and salt, stirring until butter is melted. Stir in maple flavor and vanilla. Serve warm. Refrigerate leftovers.

MAKES ABOUT 1⅓ CUPS SAUCE

Chocolate French Toast

makes 8 to 10 pieces French toast

3	eggs
¾	cup milk
3	tablespoons sugar
2	tablespoons HERSHEY'S Cocoa
¼	teaspoon vanilla extract
⅛	teaspoon salt
¼	teaspoon cinnamon (optional)
8	to 10 pieces thickly sliced bread
	Powdered sugar (optional)
	Pancake syrup (optional)

1. Beat eggs, milk, sugar, cocoa, vanilla, salt and cinnamon, if desired, in medium bowl until smooth.

2. Heat griddle or skillet over medium-low heat. Grease griddle with butter or margarine, if necessary.

3. Dip bread in egg mixture. Place on griddle. Cook about 4 minutes on each side. Serve immediately with powdered sugar or pancake syrup, if desired. Garnish as desired.

HERSHEY'S® KISSES® Birthday Cake

makes 10 to 12 servings

2 cups sugar

1¾ cups all-purpose flour

¾ cup HERSHEY'S Cocoa or HERSHEY'S SPECIAL DARK Cocoa

1½ teaspoons baking powder

1½ teaspoons baking soda

1 teaspoon salt

2 eggs

1 cup milk

½ cup vegetable oil

2 teaspoons vanilla extract

1 cup boiling water
VANILLA BUTTERCREAM FROSTING (recipe follows)
HERSHEY'S KISSES BRAND Milk Chocolates

1. Heat oven to 350°F. Grease and flour two 9-inch round baking pans or one 13×9×2-inch baking pan.

2. Stir together sugar, flour, cocoa, baking powder, baking soda and salt in large bowl. Add eggs, milk, oil and vanilla; beat with electric mixer on medium speed for 2 minutes. Stir in boiling water (batter will be thin). Pour batter into prepared pans.

3. Bake 30 to 35 minutes for round pans, 35 to 40 minutes for rectangular pan or until wooden pick inserted in center comes out clean. Cool 10 minutes; turn out onto wire racks. Cool completely.

4. Frost with VANILLA BUTTERCREAM FROSTING. Remove wrappers from chocolates. Garnish top and sides of cake with chocolates.

Vanilla Buttercream Frosting

⅓ cup butter or margarine, softened

4 cups powdered sugar, divided

3 to 4 tablespoons milk

1½ teaspoons vanilla extract

Beat butter with electric mixer on medium speed in large bowl until creamy. With mixer running, gradually add about 2 cups powdered sugar, beating until well blended. Slowly beat in milk and vanilla. Gradually add remaining powdered sugar, beating until smooth. Add additional milk, if necessary, until frosting is desired consistency.

MAKES ABOUT 2⅓ CUPS FROSTING.

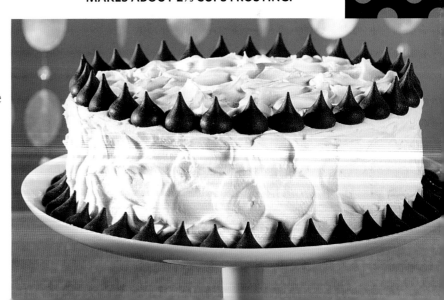

Peanut Butter Blossoms

makes about 48 cookies

48	HERSHEY'S KISSES BRAND Milk Chocolates
¾	cup REESE'S Creamy Peanut Butter
½	cup shortening
⅓	cup granulated sugar
⅓	cup packed light brown sugar
1	egg
2	tablespoons milk
1	teaspoon vanilla extract
1½	cups all-purpose flour
1	teaspoon baking soda
½	teaspoon salt
	Additional granulated sugar

1. Heat oven to 375°F. Remove wrappers from chocolates.

2. Beat peanut butter and shortening with electric mixer on medium speed in large bowl until well blended. Add ⅓ cup granulated sugar and brown sugar; beat until fluffy. Add egg, milk and vanilla; beat well. Stir together flour, baking soda and salt; gradually beat into peanut butter mixture.

3. Shape dough into 1-inch balls. Roll in additional granulated sugar; place on ungreased cookie sheet.

4. Bake 8 to 10 minutes or until lightly browned. Immediately press a chocolate into center of each cookie; cookies will crack around edges. Remove to wire racks and cool completely.

Cookie Pizza

makes about 12 slices

1   package (16 to 18 ounces) refrigerated sugar cookie dough

12   assorted HERSHEY'S MINIATURES Chocolate Bars, unwrapped

¼   cup HERSHEY'S SPECIAL DARK Chocolate Chips, HERSHEY'S Semi-Sweet Chocolate Chips or HERSHEY'S Milk Chocolate Chips

¼   cup REESE'S Peanut Butter Chips

¼   cup HERSHEY'S Premier White Chips

1   bag (10½ ounces) miniature marshmallows

¼   cup HERSHEY'S MILK DUDS Candy made with chocolate and caramels

1. Heat oven to 350°F. Press cookie dough evenly into 11-inch circle on ungreased cookie sheet. Bake 15 to 17 minutes or until lightly browned. Meanwhile, break or cut chocolate bars into about ¼-inch pieces.

2. Remove cookie from oven. Evenly sprinkle surface with chocolate chips, peanut butter chips, white chips and chocolate bar pieces. Cover "toppings" with marshmallows. Sprinkle surface with chocolate-covered caramel candies. Return to oven; bake additional 5 minutes or until marshmallows are puffed and lightly browned. Cool. Cut into triangles.

Fluffy Flavored Pancakes

makes about 14 pancakes

2 cups all-purpose biscuit baking mix

¾ cup milk

¼ cup HERSHEY'S Syrup or HERSHEY'S Strawberry Syrup

2 eggs

CHOCOLATE-MAPLE BREAKFAST SYRUP (recipe follows) or HERSHEY'S Strawberry Syrup

Stir baking mix, milk, chocolate syrup and eggs until blended in large bowl (batter will be thin). Pour batter by scant ¼ cupfuls onto hot griddle; cook until edges are dry. Turn; cook until lightly browned. Serve with CHOCOLATE-MAPLE BREAKFAST SYRUP or strawberry syrup.

Chocolate-Maple Breakfast Syrup:
Combine ½ cup HERSHEY'S Syrup or HERSHEY'S SPECIAL DARK Syrup and ½ cup maple-flavored pancake syrup. Cover; refrigerate leftover syrup. Makes 1 cup syrup.

Chocolate Quicky Sticky Bread

makes 12 servings

2 loaves (16 ounces each) frozen bread dough

¾ cup granulated sugar

1 tablespoon HERSHEY'S Cocoa

1 teaspoon ground cinnamon

½ cup (1 stick) butter or margarine, melted and divided

½ cup packed light brown sugar

¼ cup water

About 1 cup HERSHEY'S MINI KISSESBRAND Milk Chocolates

1. Thaw loaves as directed on package; let rise until doubled.

2. Stir together granulated sugar, cocoa and cinnamon. Stir together ¼ cup butter, brown sugar and water in small microwave-safe bowl. Microwave at MEDIUM (50%) 30 to 60 seconds or until smooth when stirred. Pour mixture into 12-cup fluted tube pan.

3. Heat oven to 350°F. Pinch off pieces of bread dough; form into balls (1½ inches in diameter) placing 3 chocolate pieces inside each ball. Dip each ball in remaining ¼ cup butter; roll in cocoa-sugar mixture. Place balls in prepared pan.

4. Bake 45 to 50 minutes or until golden brown. Cool 20 minutes in pan; invert onto serving plate. Cool until lukewarm.

Rich Cocoa Fudge

makes about 3 dozen pieces or 1 ¾ pounds

3 cups sugar

⅔ cup **HERSHEY'S Cocoa or HERSHEY'S SPECIAL DARK Cocoa**

⅛ teaspoon salt

1½ cups milk

¼ cup (½ stick) butter

1 teaspoon vanilla extract

1. Line 8- or 9-inch square pan with foil; extending foil over edges of pan. Butter foil.

2. Stir together sugar, cocoa and salt in heavy 4-quart saucepan; stir in milk. Cook over medium heat, stirring constantly, until mixture comes to full rolling boil. Boil, without stirring, until mixture reaches 234°F on candy thermometer or until small amount of mixture dropped into very cold water forms a soft ball which flattens when removed from water. (Bulb of candy thermometer should not rest on bottom of saucepan.) Remove from heat.

3. Add butter and vanilla. DO NOT STIR. Cool at room temperature to 110°F (lukewarm). Beat with wooden spoon until fudge thickens and just begins to lose some of its gloss. Quickly spread in prepared pan; cool completely. Cut into squares. Store in tightly covered container at room temperature.

Nutty Rich Cocoa Fudge: Beat cooked fudge as directed. Immediately stir in 1 cup chopped almonds, pecans or walnuts and quickly spread in prepared pan.

Marshmallow Nut Cocoa Fudge: Increase cocoa to ¾ cup. Cook fudge as directed. Add 1 cup marshmallow creme with butter and vanilla. DO NOT STIR. Cool to 110°F (lukewarm). Beat 8 minutes; stir in 1 cup chopped nuts. Pour into prepared pan. (Fudge does not set until poured into pan.)

Note: For best results, do not double this recipe. This is one of our most requested recipes, but also one of our most difficult. The directions must be followed exactly. Beat too little and the fudge is too soft. Beat too long and it becomes hard and sugary.

Chocolate-Covered Banana Pops

makes 9 pops

3 ripe large bananas

9 wooden ice cream sticks

2 cups (12-ounce package) HERSHEY'S SPECIAL DARK Chocolate Chips or HERSHEY'S Semi-Sweet Chocolate Chips

2 tablespoons shortening (do not use butter, margarine, spread or oil)

1½ cups coarsely chopped unsalted, roasted peanuts

Variation: HERSHEY'S Milk Chocolate Chips or HERSHEY'S Mini Chips Semi-Sweet Chocolate may be substituted for HERSHEY'S SPECIAL DARK Chocolate Chips or HERSHEY'S Semi-Sweet Chocolate Chips.

1. Peel bananas; cut each into thirds. Insert a wooden stick into each banana piece; place on wax paper-covered tray. Cover; freeze until firm.

2. Place chocolate chips and shortening in medium microwave-safe bowl. Microwave at MEDIUM (50%) 1½ to 2 minutes or until chocolate is melted and mixture is smooth when stirred.

3. Remove bananas from freezer just before dipping. Dip each piece into warm chocolate, covering completely; allow excess to drip off. Immediately roll in peanuts. Cover; return to freezer. Serve frozen.

Fun *and* Games

Dutch Country Dirt

makes 1 serving

Chocolate wafer cookies

2   to 3 tablespoons HERSHEY'S Syrup

2   scoops (about ½ cup each) chocolate ice cream, softened

½   cup HERSHEY'S MINI KISSES BRAND Milk Chocolates

1   tablespoon HERSHEY'S Cocoa or HERSHEY'S SPECIAL DARK Cocoa

1   tablespoon powdered sugar

1. Crush 1 to 2 cookies; place on bottom of ice cream dish. Cover cookies with chocolate syrup.

2. Combine 1 scoop chocolate ice cream with chocolate pieces; place on top of cookies and syrup. Top with second scoop chocolate ice cream.

3. Stir together cocoa and powdered sugar; sprinkle over ice cream. Garnish as desired.

Peanut Butter and Milk Chocolate Chip Cattails

makes 12 to 14 coated pretzels

1   **cup HERSHEY'S Milk Chocolate Chips, divided**

1   **cup REESE'S Peanut Butter Chips, divided**

2   **teaspoons shortening (do not use butter, margarine, spread or oil)**

12   **to 14 pretzel rods**

1. Stir together milk chocolate chips and peanut butter chips. Place sheet of wax paper on tray or counter top. Finely chop 1 cup chip mixture in food processor or by hand; place on wax paper. Line tray or cookie sheet with wax paper.

2. Place remaining 1 cup chip mixture and shortening in narrow deep microwave-safe bowl. Microwave at MEDIUM (50%) 1 minute; stir. If necessary, microwave additional 15 seconds at a time, stirring after each heating, until chips are melted and mixture is smooth when stirred.

3. Spoon chocolate-peanut butter mixture over about ¾ of pretzel rod; gently shake off excess. Holding pretzel by uncoated end, roll in chopped chips, pressing chips into chocolate. Place on prepared tray. Refrigerate 30 minutes or until set. Store coated pretzels in cool, dry place.

Variation: Melt 1 cup milk chocolate chips and 1 cup peanut butter chips with 4 teaspoons shortening; dip small pretzels into mixture.

Brownie Surprise Pops

makes about 36 pops

1	(13×9×2-inch) pan fudgey brownie from mix or your favorite recipe
1⅓	cups (8-ounce package) REESE'S Minis Peanut Butter Cups, divided
2	cups (11.5-ounce package) HERSHEY'S Milk Chocolate Chips, divided
36	lollipop sticks
	Styrofoam block
2	cups (12-ounce package) HERSHEY'S Premier White Chips
	ROYAL ICING (recipe follows)
	Food colors
	Small candy garnishes (optional)

1. Following package or recipe directions, prepare and bake brownies in foil-lined pan with foil extending beyond pan edges. Cool completely in pan.

2. Using foil as handles, lift brownie out of pan. Cut off brownie edges. With hands, knead and roll remaining brownie until it forms one large ball. Divide brownie ball into 36 (about 1¼-inch) balls. Flatten each ball slightly; press around one mini peanut butter cup, forming ball and covering peanut butter cup completely.

3. Place ¼ cup milk chocolate chips in small microwave-safe bowl. Microwave at

MEDIUM (50%) 30 seconds; stir. If necessary, microwave at MEDIUM an additional 10 seconds at a time, stirring after each heating, until chips are melted and smooth when stirred. One at a time, dip about ½ inch of the tip of a lollipop stick into melted chocolate and insert stick about halfway into brownie ball. Insert lollipop stick into styrofoam block. Repeat procedure with remaining brownie balls. Cover with plastic wrap and refrigerate several hours or until balls are firm.

4. Place white chips and remaining milk chocolate chips in deep microwave-safe bowl (such as large glass measuring cup). Microwave at MEDIUM 1 minute; stir. If necessary, microwave at MEDIUM an additional 15 seconds at a time, stirring after each heating, until chips are melted and smooth when stirred.

5. Dip brownie pop into melted chocolate mixture; gently tap off excess coating. Insert coated pop back into styrofoam block. (Peanut butter cup ears or noses can be added before coating sets up or can be added later with a bit of melted chocolate or icing.) Repeat until all pops are coated. If coating mixture cools and coating becomes difficult, microwave at MEDIUM 10 to 15 seconds; stir.) Allow coating to set before decorating.

fun and games

6. Prepare ROYAL ICING. Decorate brownie pops as desired with prepared icing and garnishes. Use icing to "glue" small candies or garnishes to pops. Allow icing to harden. (If you don't like the design or parts of the design, wait until the icing has hardened and then you can remove without damaging the surface of the pop.) Store decorated pops in a cool, dry place.

Royal Icing: Stir together 2¼ cups powdered sugar, 2 tablespoons warm water and 1 tablespoon pasteurized dried egg whites (meringue powder). Beat at medium speed of electric mixer until spreadable. Add additional water, 1 teaspoon at a time, if too thick. Divide icing into small bowls for each color desired and tint with food colorings. Transfer icing to pastry bags with desired tip. Cover icings and tips of pastry bags with damp paper towels to keep icing from drying out. (Some garnishes may need a firmer icing to hold their shape. Stir in small amounts of additional powdered sugar to get desired consistency.) Makes 1 cup icing.

Chocolate Cookie Pretzels

makes 24 cookies

⅔ cup butter or margarine, softened

1 cup granulated sugar

2 teaspoons vanilla extract

2 eggs

2½ cups all-purpose flour

½ cup HERSHEY'S Cocoa

½ teaspoon baking soda

¼ teaspoon salt

Powdered sugar or SATINY CHOCOLATE GLAZE or PEANUT BUTTER CHIP FROSTING (recipes follow, optional)

1. Heat oven to 350°F.

2. Beat butter, granulated sugar and vanilla in large bowl until fluffy. Add eggs; beat well. Stir together flour, cocoa, baking soda and salt; gradually add to butter mixture, beating until well blended.

3. Divide dough into 24 pieces. On lightly floured surface, roll each piece with hands into pencil-like strip, about 12 inches long. Place strip on ungreased cookie sheet. Twist into pretzel shape by crossing left side of strip to middle, forming loop. Fold right side up and over first loop. Place about 2 inches apart on cookie sheet.

4. Bake 8 minutes or until set. Cool 1 minute; remove from cookie sheet to wire rack. Cool completely. Sprinkle with powdered sugar, if desired, or frost with SATINY CHOCOLATE GLAZE or PEANUT BUTTER CHIP FROSTING.

Satiny Chocolate Glaze

2 tablespoons butter or margarine

3 tablespoons HERSHEY'S Cocoa

2 tablespoons water

½ teaspoon vanilla extract

1 cup powdered sugar

1. Melt butter in small saucepan over low heat; add cocoa and water. Cook, stirring constantly, until mixture thickens; do not boil. Remove from heat; stir in vanilla.

2. Gradually add powdered sugar, beating with whisk until smooth. Add additional water, ½ teaspoon at a time, until glaze is of desired consistency.

MAKES ABOUT ¾ CUP GLAZE

Peanut Butter Chip Frosting

1	cup powdered sugar
¼	cup (½ stick) butter or margarine
3	tablespoons milk
1	cup REESE'S Peanut Butter Chips
½	teaspoon vanilla extract

1. Measure powdered sugar into medium bowl; set aside. Combine butter, milk and peanut butter chips in small saucepan; cook over low heat, stirring constantly, until chips are melted and mixture is smooth. Remove from heat.

2. Add warm mixture to powdered sugar; stir in vanilla. Beat until smooth. Spread while frosting is warm.

MAKES ABOUT 1 CUP FROSTING

Cheery Chocolate Teddy Bear Cookies

makes about 48 cookies

1⅔ cups (10-ounce) package REESE'S Peanut Butter Chips

1 cup HERSHEY'S SPECIAL DARK Chocolate Chips or HERSHEY'S Semi-Sweet Chocolate Chips

2 tablespoons shortening (do not use butter, margarine, spread or oil)

1 package (20 ounces) chocolate sandwich cookies

1 package (10 ounces) teddy bear shaped graham snack crackers

1. Line tray or cookie sheet with wax paper.

2. Combine chips and shortening in 2-quart glass measuring cup with handle. Microwave at MEDIUM (50%) 1½ to 2 minutes or until chips are melted and mixture is smooth when stirred. Using fork, dip each cookie into chip mixture; gently tap fork on side of cup to remove excess chocolate.

3. Place coated cookies on prepared tray; top each cookie with a graham snack cracker. Chill until chocolate is set, about 30 minutes. Store in airtight container in a cool, dry place.

fun and games

Chocolate X and O Cookies

makes about 5 dozen cookies

⅔	cup butter or margarine, softened
1	cup sugar
2	teaspoons vanilla extract
2	eggs
2	tablespoons light corn syrup
2½	cups all-purpose flour
½	cup HERSHEY'S Cocoa
½	teaspoon baking soda
¼	teaspoon salt
	Decorating icing

1. Beat butter, sugar and vanilla in large bowl on medium speed of mixer until fluffy. Add eggs; beat well. Beat in corn syrup.

2. Combine flour, cocoa, baking soda and salt; gradually add to butter mixture, beating until well blended. Cover; refrigerate until dough is firm enough to handle.

3. Heat oven to 350°F. Shape dough into X and O shapes.* Place on ungreased cookie sheet.

4. Bake 5 minutes or until set. Remove from cookie sheet to wire rack. Cool completely. Decorate as desired with icing.

*To shape X's: Shape rounded teaspoons of dough into 3-inch logs. Place 1 log on cookie sheet; press lightly in center. Place another 3-inch log on top of first one, forming X shape. To shape O's: Shape rounded teaspoons of dough into 5-inch logs. Connect ends, pressing lightly, forming O shape.

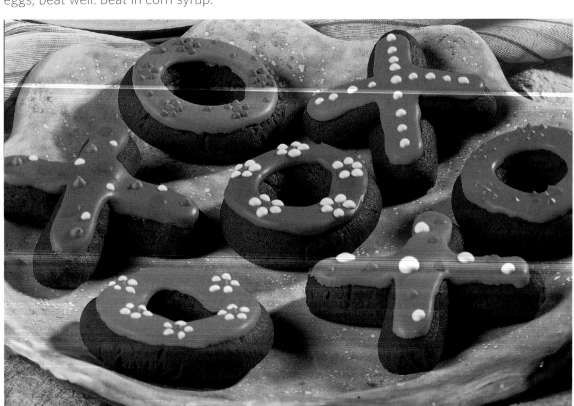

Edible "Masks"

makes 2 cookies

1   package (16 to 18 ounces) refrigerated sugar cookie dough

¾   cup all-purpose flour

1   can (16 ounces) vanilla ready-to-spread frosting

      Assorted food color

      Decorations, such as ROLO Chewy Caramels in Milk Chocolate, HERSHEY'S KISSESBRAND Milk Chocolates, YORK Peppermint Patties, KIT KAT Wafer Bars, REESE'S PIECES Candies, TWIZZLERS PULL-N-PEEL Candy

1. Heat oven to 350°F. Grease cookie sheet or line with parchment paper.

2. Combine cookie dough and flour until mixture holds together. Roll dough into ¼-inch-thick rectangle on lightly floured work surface.

3. Draw two (7- to 8-inch-high) Halloween shapes (pumpkin, ghost, witch, etc.) on cardboard; cut out. Cover them with clear plastic wrap. Place over dough; trace around cardboard pattern with knife. Cut completely through dough. Place shapes on prepared cookie sheet. Using a straw, make one (¼-inch-wide) hole in each side of "mask" where ear would be.

4. Bake 15 to 20 minutes or until lightly browned. (If necessary, re-cut holes on both sides of mask while cookie is still hot. Cool slightly; carefully remove from cookie sheet to wire rack. Cool completely.

5. Divide frosting and tint with food color; frost cookies. Using your imagination, decorate cookies with assorted candies. Separate PULL-N-PEEL candy into strands; tie 1 strand into each hole to resemble strings on a mask.

Chocolate Barbeque Grill Cake

makes 15 servings

1   cup water
1   cup (2 sticks) butter or margarine
½   cup HERSHEY'S Cocoa
2   cups sugar
1¾   cups all-purpose flour
1   teaspoon baking soda
½   teaspoon salt
3   eggs
¾   cup dairy sour cream
⅔   cup REESE'S Peanut Butter Chips
1   teaspoon shortening (do not use butter, margarine, spread or oil)
    COCOA FUDGE "BURGERS" (recipe follows, optional)
    Fruit shaped gumdrop candies (optional)

1. Heat oven to 350°F. Line 13×9×2-inch baking pan with foil; grease and flour sides and bottom.

2. Place water, butter and cocoa in medium saucepan. Cook over medium heat, stirring occasionally, until mixture boils; boil 1 minute. Remove from heat; set aside.

3. Stir together sugar, flour, baking soda and salt in large bowl. Add eggs, sour cream and cocoa mixture; beat just until blended (batter will be thin). Pour into prepared pan.

4. Bake 45 to 50 minutes or until wooden pick inserted in center comes out clean. Cool cake completely in pan on wire rack. Carefully invert cake onto serving tray; peel off foil.

5. Place peanut butter chips and shortening in small microwave-safe bowl. Microwave at MEDIUM (50%) 30 to 45 seconds or until mixture is melted when stirred. Place mixture in recloseable food storage bag; cut off tiny section of corner. Squeeze mixture onto cake, forming grids like top of grill; allow to firm up before cutting. Top with "burgers" and "shish kabobs," if desired.

Cocoa Fudge "Burgers": Beat ¼ cup softened butter or margarine in medium bowl; add 2 cups powdered sugar, ½ cup HERSHEY'S Cocoa, 2 tablespoons milk and ½ teaspoon vanilla extract. Beat until all ingredients are moistened and consistency to form patties; add additional milk or powdered sugar, if necessary, to get proper consistency. Form "patties"; place on top of cake.

"Shish Kabobs": Place red, green and tan colored jelly candies on plastic decorative skewers to form shish kabobs, if desired. Place on top of cake.

chock-full of Gifts

White Chip and Macadamia Toffee Crunch

makes 1 pound candy

1	cup HERSHEY'S Premier White Chips
½	cup MAUNA LOA Macadamia Nut Baking Pieces
¾	cup (1½ sticks) butter
¾	cup sugar
3	tablespoons light corn syrup

1. Line 8- or 9-inch square or round pan with foil, extending foil over edges of pan; butter foil. Stir together white chips and nuts. Reserve 2 tablespoons white chip and nut mixture; sprinkle remaining chip mixture over bottom of prepared pan.

2. Combine butter, sugar and corn syrup in heavy medium saucepan; cook over low heat, stirring constantly, until butter is melted and sugar is dissolved. Increase heat to medium; cook, stirring constantly, until mixture boils. Cook and stir until mixture turns a medium caramel color (about 15 minutes).

3. Immediately pour mixture over chip and nut mixture in pan, spreading evenly. Sprinkle reserved chip mixture over surface. Cool. Refrigerate until chips are firm. Remove from pan; peel off foil. Break into pieces. Store tightly covered in cool, dry place.

Dark Chocolate and Macadamia Toffee Crunch: Substitute 1 cup HERSHEY'S SPECIAL DARK Chocolate Chips for HERSHEY'S Premier White Chips.

Chocolate Buttercream Cherry Candies

makes about 48 candies

About 48 maraschino cherries with stems, well drained

¼   cup (½ stick) butter, softened

2   cups powdered sugar

¼   cup HERSHEY'S Cocoa or HERSHEY'S SPECIAL DARK Cocoa

1   to 2 tablespoons milk, divided

½   teaspoon vanilla extract

¼   teaspoon almond extract

WHITE CHIP COATING (recipe follows)

CHOCOLATE CHIP DRIZZLE (recipe follows)

1. Cover tray with wax paper. Lightly press cherries between layers of paper towels to remove excess moisture.

2. Beat butter, powdered sugar, cocoa and 1 tablespoon milk in small bowl until well blended; stir in vanilla and almond extract. If necessary, add remaining milk, 1 teaspoon at a time, until mixture will hold together but is not wet.

3. Mold scant teaspoon mixture around each cherry, covering completely; place on prepared tray. Cover; refrigerate 3 hours or until firm.

4. Prepare WHITE CHIP COATING. Holding each cherry by stem, dip into coating. Place on tray; refrigerate until firm.

5. About 1 hour before serving, prepare CHOCOLATE CHIP DRIZZLE; with tines of fork drizzle randomly over candies. Refrigerate until drizzle is firm. Store in refrigerator.

White Chip Coating: Place 2 cups (12-ounce package) HERSHEY'S Premier White Chips in small microwave-safe bowl; drizzle with 2 tablespoons vegetable oil. Microwave at MEDIUM (50%) 1 minute; stir. If necessary, microwave at MEDIUM an additional 15 seconds at a time, stirring after each heating, just until chips are melted and mixture is smooth. If mixture thickens while coating, microwave at MEDIUM 15 seconds; stir until smooth.

Chocolate Chip Drizzle: Place ¼ cup HERSHEY'S SPECIAL DARK Chocolate Chips or HERSHEY'S Semi-Sweet Chocolate Chips and ¼ teaspoon shortening (do not use butter, margarine, spread or oil) in another small microwave-safe bowl. Microwave at MEDIUM (50%) 30 seconds to 1 minute; stir until chips are melted and mixture is smooth.

chock-full of gifts

Gumdrop Bark

makes about 1 pound candy

About ¼ cup red spice gumdrops*

About ¼ cup green spice gumdrops*

2   cups (12-ounce package) HERSHEY'S Premier White Chips

Amounts and gumdrop flavors can vary according to your own preference.

1. Line cookie sheet with wax paper. Cut gumdrops into slices about ¼-inch thick; set aside.

2. Place white chips in medium microwave-safe bowl. Microwave at MEDIUM (50%) 1 minute; stir. Continue microwaving at MEDIUM in 15-second increments, stirring after each heating, until chips are melted and smooth when stirred.

3. Pour melted chips onto prepared cookie sheet; spread to about ½-inch thickness. Gently tap cookie sheet on countertop to even out thickness of melted chips. Sprinkle gumdrop slices over surface. Repeat tapping cookie sheet on counter until candy is desired thickness.

4. Refrigerate about 30 minutes or until firm. Break into pieces. Store in cool, dry place.

Peanut Butter Cup Surprise Truffles

makes about 42 truffles

2   packages (11.5 ounces each) HERSHEY'S Milk Chocolate Chips, divided

¾   cup whipping cream

1⅓   cups (8-ounce package) REESE'S Minis Peanut Butter Cups

2   cups (12-ounce package) HERSHEY'S Premier White Chips, divided

1. Place 3 cups milk chocolate chips and whipping cream in large microwave-safe container. Microwave at MEDIUM (50%) 1 minute; stir. If necessary, microwave at MEDIUM an additional 15 seconds at a time, stirring after each heating, until chips are melted and mixture is smooth when stirred. Cover; refrigerate several hours or until firm.

2. Line cookie sheet or tray with wax paper. Roll mixture into 1-inch balls; place on prepared tray. Refrigerate about 1 hour or until firm enough to handle.

3. Flatten each ball slightly; press around 1 mini peanut butter cup, covering cup completely. Return to tray. Cover; refrigerate about 30 minutes.

4. Line second cookie sheet or tray with wax paper or line candy cups on tray, if desired. Place remaining 1 cup milk chocolate chips and 1¼ cups white chips in medium microwave-safe bowl. Microwave at MEDIUM 1 minute; stir. If necessary, microwave at MEDIUM an additional 15 seconds at a time, stirring after each heating, just until chips are melted and smooth when stirred.

5. Place truffle on fork and immediately dip into melted chocolate mixture; allow excess chocolate to drip off truffles. If necessary, scrape off excess chocolate with knife or small spatula. Place on prepared tray or in paper cups. Refrigerate until coating is firm (about 30 minutes).

6. Place remaining ¾ cup white chips in small microwave-safe bowl. Microwave at MEDIUM 1 minute; stir. If necessary, microwave at MEDIUM an additional 15 seconds at a time, stirring after each heating, until chips are melted and smooth when stirred. Transfer melted chips to heavy duty (freezer) resealable food storage bag. Cut tip of bag about ⅛th inch from corner; drizzle melted white chips in decorative design on tops of truffles. Allow to set. Store in cool, dry place.

chock-full of gifts

Peanut Butter Chip Brittle

makes about 2 pounds candy

1²⁄₃	**cups (10-ounce package) REESE'S Peanut Butter Chips, divided**
1½	**cups (3 sticks) butter or margarine**
1¾	**cups sugar**
3	**tablespoons light corn syrup**
3	**tablespoons water**

1. Butter 15½×10½×1-inch jelly-roll pan.* Sprinkle 1 cup peanut butter chips evenly onto bottom of prepared pan; set aside.

2. Melt butter in heavy 2½-quart saucepan; stir in sugar, corn syrup and water. Cook over medium heat, stirring constantly, until mixture reaches 300°F on candy thermometer. (This should take 30 to 35 minutes. Bulb of thermometer should not rest on bottom of saucepan.)

3. Remove from heat. Immediately spread mixture in prepared pan; sprinkle with remaining ²⁄₃ cup peanut butter chips. Cool completely. Remove from pan. Break into pieces. Store in tightly covered container in cool, dry place.

For thicker brittle, use a 13×9-inch pan.--

chock-full of gifts

Jingle Bells Chocolate Pretzels

makes about 24 coated pretzels

1 cup HERSHEY'S SPECIAL DARK Chocolate Chips or HERSHEY'S Semi-Sweet Chocolate Chips

1 cup HERSHEY'S Premier White Chips, divided

1 tablespoon plus ½ teaspoon shortening (do not use butter, margarine, spread or oil), divided

About 24 salted or unsalted pretzels (3×2 inches)

1. Cover tray or cookie sheet with wax paper.

2. Place chocolate chips, ⅔ cup white chips and 1 tablespoon shortening in medium microwave-safe bowl. Microwave at MEDIUM (50%) 1 minute; stir. Microwave at MEDIUM an additional 1 to 2 minutes, stirring every 30 seconds, until chips are melted when stirred.

3. Using fork, dip each pretzel into chocolate mixture; tap fork on side of bowl to remove excess chocolate. Place coated pretzels on prepared tray.

4. Place remaining ⅓ cup white chips and remaining ½ teaspoon shortening in small microwave-safe bowl. Microwave at MEDIUM 15 to 30 seconds or until chips are melted when stirred. Using tines of fork, drizzle chip mixture across pretzels. Refrigerate until coating is set. Store in airtight container in cool, dry place.

White Dipped Pretzels: Cover tray with wax paper. Place 2 cups (12-ounce package) HERSHEY'S Premier White Chips and 2 tablespoons shortening (do not use butter, margarine, spread or oil) in medium microwave-safe bowl. Microwave at MEDIUM 1 to 2 minutes or until chips are melted when stirred. Dip pretzels as directed above. Place ¼ cup HERSHEY'S SPECIAL DARK Chocolate Chips or HERSHEY'S Semi-Sweet Chocolate Chips and ¼ teaspoon shortening (do not use butter, margarine, spread or oil) in small microwave-safe bowl. Microwave at MEDIUM 30 seconds to 1 minute or until chips are melted when stirred. Drizzle melted chocolate across pretzels, using tines of fork. Refrigerate and store as directed above.

White Chip Trail Mix

makes about 11½ cups snack mix

½	cup (1 stick) butter or margarine, melted
2	tablespoons HERSHEY'S Cocoa
2	tablespoons sugar
4	cups toasted oat cereal rings
4	cups bite-size crisp wheat squares cereal
1	cup slivered almonds
1	cup golden raisins
2	cups (12-ounce package) HERSHEY'S Premier White Chips

1. Heat oven to 250°F.

2. Stir together butter, cocoa and sugar in small bowl. Combine cereals and almonds in large bowl; stir in butter mixture. Toss until ingredients are well coated. Pour mixture into 13×9×2-inch baking pan.

3. Bake 1 hour, stirring every 15 minutes. Cool completely; stir in raisins and white chips. Store in tightly covered container in cool, dry place.

Microwave Directions: Place margarine in 4-quart microwave-safe bowl. Microwave at HIGH (100%) 1 minute or until melted; stir in cocoa and sugar. Add cereals and almonds; stir until evenly coated. Microwave at HIGH 3 minutes, stirring every minute; stir in raisins. Microwave at HIGH additional 3 minutes, stirring every minute. Cool completely; stir in white chips. Store in tightly covered container in cool, dry place.

HERSHEY'S® BAKING MELTS® Sandwich Cookies

*makes about 48 sandwich cookies**

¾   **cup (1½ sticks) butter or margarine, softened**

1   **cup sugar**

1   **egg**

½   **teaspoon vanilla extract**

1½   **cups all-purpose flour**

½   **teaspoon baking soda**

¼   **teaspoon salt**

1¾   **cups (10-ounce package) HERSHEY'S BAKING MELTS Semi-Sweet Chocolate or (9.5-ounce package) HERSHEY'S BAKING MELTS Milk Chocolate**

1. Heat oven to 350°F.

2. Beat butter and sugar in large bowl until well blended. Add egg and vanilla; beat well. Stir together flour, baking soda and salt; gradually add to butter mixture, beating until blended. Shape dough into ¾-inch balls (about 1 measuring teaspoon dough). Place balls on ungreased cookie sheet.

3. Bake 8 to 10 minutes or until edges are lightly browned and cookies are set. Cool slightly; remove cookies from sheet to wire rack. Cool completely.

4. Heat oven to 200°F. Line jelly-roll pan or cookie sheet with parchment paper. Working with a dozen cookies at a time, place half of the baked cookies on prepared pan with bottom side of cookie up. Stack 2 chocolate pieces on each cookie.

5. Heat cookies and chocolate 5 to 7 minutes or until chocolate is melted and can be spread with small spatula. (Do not overheat. Melted chocolate retains its shape until disturbed.) Spread melted chocolate to cover surface of cookie; top with second cookie. Allow cookies to cool until chocolate is set.

There may be extra single cookies.

chock-full of gifts

Creamy Double Decker Fudge

makes about 4 dozen pieces or 1½ pounds candy

1   cup REESE'S Peanut Butter Chips

1   can (14 ounces) sweetened condensed milk (not evaporated milk), divided

1   teaspoon vanilla extract, divided

1   cup HERSHEY'S SPECIAL DARK Chocolate Chips or HERSHEY'S Semi-Sweet Chocolate Chips

1. Line 8-inch square pan with foil.

2. Place peanut butter chips and ½ cup sweetened condensed milk in small microwave-safe bowl. Microwave at HIGH (100%) 1 to 1½ minutes, stirring after 1 minute, until chips are melted and mixture is smooth when stirred. Stir in ½ teaspoon vanilla; spread evenly in prepared pan.

3. Place remaining sweetened condensed milk and chocolate chips in another small microwave-safe bowl; repeat above microwave procedure. Stir in remaining ½ teaspoon vanilla; spread evenly over peanut butter layer.

4. Cover; refrigerate until firm. Remove from pan; place on cutting board. Peel off foil. Cut into squares. Store tightly covered in refrigerator.

Note: For best results, do not double this recipe.

56

chock-full of gifts

Classic MINI KISSES® Cookie Mix
(Cookie Mix in a Jar)

makes 1 jar mix

2¼ cups all-purpose flour

⅔ cup granulated sugar

1 teaspoon baking soda

½ teaspoon salt

1½ cups HERSHEY'S MINI KISSESBRAND Milk Chocolates, divided

⅔ cup packed light brown sugar
 BAKING INSTRUCTIONS (recipe follows)

1. Stir together flour, granulated sugar, baking soda and salt. Transfer mixture to clean 1-quart (4-cup) glass jar with lid; pack down into bottom of jar.

2. Layer with 1 cup chocolate pieces and brown sugar.* Top with remaining ½ cup chocolates; close jar. Attach card with BAKING INSTRUCTIONS.

To increase shelf life of mix, wrap brown sugar in plastic wrap and press into place.

Tip: For best results, use cookie mix within 4 weeks of assembly.

Classic MINI KISSES® Cookies

1 jar Classic MINI KISSESBRAND Cookie Mix

1 cup (2 sticks) butter, softened and cut into pieces

1 teaspoon vanilla extract

2 eggs, lightly beaten

Baking Instructions

1. Heat oven to 375°F.

2. Spoon contents of jar into large bowl; stir to break up any lumps. Add butter and vanilla; stir until crumbly mixture forms. Add eggs; stir to form smooth, very stiff dough. Drop by heaping teaspoons onto ungreased cookie sheet.

3. Bake 8 to 10 minutes or until lightly browned. Cool slightly; remove from cookie sheet to wire rack. Cool completely.

MAKES 36 COOKIES

no-bake Treats

Chocolate Graham Cracker Sundae

makes 1 serving

1¾   **graham crackers**

2   **tablespoons marshmallow creme**

2   **scoops (about ½ cup each) vanilla ice cream**

2   **tablespoons HERSHEY'S Syrup**

¼   **cup miniature marshmallows**

1. Place 2 halves of graham crackers in bottom of chilled bowl.

2. Spoon marshmallow creme onto each half graham cracker.

3. Place scoops of vanilla ice cream onto the marshmallow creme.

4. Top ice cream with chocolate syrup.

5. Fan the remaining three quarters of graham cracker in between the scoops of ice cream.

6. Sprinkle the marshmallows onto the chocolate syrup around the ice cream.

Chocolate-Peanut Butter Coated Apples

makes 10 to 12 apples

10   to 12 lollipop sticks

10   to 12 medium apples, stems removed

1⅔   cups (10-ounce package) REESE'S Peanut Butter Chips

½   cup vegetable oil

⅔   cup powdered sugar

⅔   cup HERSHEY'S Cocoa

    MOUNDS Sweetened Coconut Flakes or chopped REESE'S Peanut Butter Chips (optional)

1. Insert lollipop stick into each washed and dried apple. Cover tray with wax paper.

2. Stir together peanut butter chips and oil in medium microwave-safe bowl. Microwave at MEDIUM (50%) 1½ minutes or until chips are softened. Stir until melted. If necessary, microwave at MEDIUM an additional 15 seconds at a time, stirring after each heating, just until chips are melted when stirred.

3. Stir together powdered sugar and cocoa; gradually add to melted chip mixture, stirring until smooth. Microwave at MEDIUM 1 minute or until very warm.

4. Dip apples in mixture; twirl to remove excess coating. (If coating becomes too thick, return to microwave for a few seconds or add additional oil 1 teaspoon at a time.) Roll lower half of coated apple in coconut or chopped chips, if desired. Allow to cool on prepared tray. Refrigerate, if desired.

no-bake treats

Drizzled Party Popcorn

makes about 8 cups popcorn

8   cups popped popcorn
½   cup **HERSHEY'S Milk Chocolate Chips**
2   teaspoons shortening (do not use butter, margarine, spread or oil), divided
½   cup **REESE'S Peanut Butter Chips**

1. Line cookie sheet or jelly-roll pan with wax paper. Spread popcorn in thin layer on prepared pan.

2. Place milk chocolate chips and 1 teaspoon shortening in microwave-safe bowl. Microwave at MEDIUM (50%) 30 seconds; stir. If necessary, microwave at MEDIUM an additional 10 seconds at a time, stirring after each heating, until chips are melted and smooth when stirred. Drizzle over popcorn.

3. Place peanut butter chips and remaining 1 teaspoon shortening in separate microwave-safe bowl. Microwave at MEDIUM 30 seconds; stir. If necessary, microwave at MEDIUM an additional 10 seconds at a time, stirring after each heating, until chips are melted and smooth when stirred. Drizzle over popcorn.

4. Allow drizzle to set up at room temperature or refrigerate about 10 minutes or until firm. Break popcorn into pieces.

Notes: Popcorn is best eaten the same day as prepared, but it can be stored in an airtight container. Recipe amounts can be changed to match your personal preferences.

Mini Chocolate Pies

makes 6 servings

1   package (4-serving size) vanilla cook & serve pudding and pie filling mix*

1   cup HERSHEY'S Mini Chips Semi-Sweet Chocolate

1   package (4 ounces) single-serve graham cracker crusts (6 crusts)

     Whipped topping

     Additional HERSHEY'S Mini Chips Semi-Sweet Chocolate, HERSHEY'S SPECIAL DARK Chocolate Chips or HERSHEY'S Semi-Sweet Chocolate Chips (optional)

Do not use instant pudding mix.

1. Prepare pudding and pie filling mix as directed on package; remove from heat. Immediately add 1 cup small chocolate chips; stir until melted. Cool 5 minutes, stirring occasionally.

2. Pour filling into crusts; press plastic wrap directly onto surface. Refrigerate several hours or until firm. Garnish with whipped topping and small chocolate chips, if desired.

Indoor or Outdoor S'mores

makes 4 servings

4   graham crackers, broken into halves

2   HERSHEY'S Milk Chocolate Bars (1.55 ounces each), broken into halves

4   marshmallows

Place 1 graham cracker half on paper towel; top with chocolate bar half and 1 marshmallow. Microwave at MEDIUM (50%) in 10-second intervals until marshmallow puffs. Immediately top with remaining graham cracker half; gently press together. Repeat for each serving; serve immediately.

Outdoor S'mores: Place ½ of HERSHEY'S Milk Chocolate Bar (1.55 ounces) on graham cracker half. Carefully toast marshmallow over grill or campfire (supervise the kids if they're doing this); place over chocolate. Top with second graham cracker half; gently press together.

no-bake treats

MINI CHOCOLATE PIES

Banana Fudge Pops

makes 6 pops

1	ripe medium banana
1½	cups orange banana juice
½	cup sugar
¼	cup HERSHEY'S Cocoa
½	cup plus 2 tablespoons (5-ounce can) evaporated milk
6	paper cold drink cups (5 ounces each)
6	wooden ice cream sticks

1. Slice banana into blender container; add juice. Cover; blend until smooth. Add sugar and cocoa; cover and blend well. Add evaporated milk; cover and blend.

2. Pour mixture into cups. Freeze about 1 hour; insert wooden sticks into fudge pops. Cover; freeze until firm. Peel off cups to serve.

no-bake treats

HERSHEY'S® Easy Chocolate Cracker Snacks

makes about 5½ dozen crackers

1⅔ cups (10-ounce package) HERSHEY'S Mint Chocolate Chips*

2 cups (12-ounce package) HERSHEY'S SPECIAL DARK Chocolate Chips or HERSHEY'S Semi-Sweet Chocolate Chips

2 tablespoons shortening (do not use butter, margarine, spread or oil)

60 to 70 round buttery crackers (about one-half 1-pound box)

2 cups (11.5-ounce package) HERSHEY'S Milk Chocolate Chips and ¼ teaspoon pure peppermint extract can be substituted for mint chocolate chips.

1. Line several trays or cookie sheets with wax paper.

2. Place mint chocolate chips, chocolate chips and shortening in large microwave-safe bowl. Microwave at MEDIUM (50%) 1 minute; stir. Continue heating 30 seconds at a time, stirring after each heating, until chips are melted and mixture is smooth when stirred.

3. Drop crackers into chocolate mixture one at a time. Using tongs, push cracker into chocolate so that it is covered completely. (If chocolate begins to thicken, reheat 10 to 20 seconds in microwave.) Remove from chocolate, tapping lightly on edge of bowl to remove excess chocolate. Place on prepared tray. Refrigerate until chocolate hardens, about 20 minutes. For best results, store tightly covered in refrigerator.

Peanut Butter and Milk Chocolate: Use 1⅔ cups (10-ounce package) REESE'S Peanut Butter Chips, 2 cups (11.5-ounce package) HERSHEY'S Milk Chocolate Chips and 2 tablespoons shortening. Proceed as directed.

White Chip and Toffee: Melt 2 bags (12 ounces each) HERSHEY'S Premier White Chips and 2 tablespoons shortening. Dip crackers; before coating hardens sprinkle with HEATH BITS 'O BRICKLE Toffee Bits.

White & Chocolate Covered Strawberries

makes 2 to 3 dozen berries

2   **cups (12-ounce package) HERSHEY'S Premier White Chips**

2   **tablespoons shortening (do not use butter, margarine, spread or oil), divided**

4   **cups (2 pints) fresh strawberries, rinsed, patted dry and chilled**

1   **cup HERSHEY'S SPECIAL DARK Chocolate Chips or HERSHEY'S Semi-Sweet Chocolate Chips**

1. Cover tray with wax paper.

2. Place white chips and 1 tablespoon shortening in medium microwave-safe bowl. Microwave at MEDIUM (50%) 1 minute; stir until chips are melted and mixture is smooth. If necessary, microwave at MEDIUM an additional 15 seconds at a time, just until smooth when stirred.

3. Holding by top, dip ⅓ of each strawberry into white chip mixture; shake gently to remove excess. Place on prepared tray; refrigerate until coating is firm, at least 30 minutes.

4. Repeat microwave procedure with chocolate chips and remaining shortening in clean microwave-safe bowl. Dip lower ⅓ of each berry into chocolate mixture. Refrigerate until firm. Cover; refrigerate leftover strawberries.

no-bake treats

Easy S'more Clusters

makes about 2½ dozen snacks

6   HERSHEY'S Milk Chocolate Bars
    (1.55 ounces each), broken into
    pieces
2   cups miniature marshmallows
8   graham crackers, coarsely chopped
    (about 1¾ cups)

1. Place candy pieces in medium microwave-safe bowl. Microwave at MEDIUM (50%) 1½ to 2 minutes, or until chocolate is melted when mixture is stirred.

2. Stir in marshmallows and graham cracker pieces until well coated. Drop by spoonfuls into miniature paper muffin cups (1¾ inches in diameter). Cover; refrigerate until firm.

Macadamia Nut Fudge

makes 2 pounds fudge

1½   **cups sugar**

1   **jar (7 ounces) marshmallow creme**

1   **can (5 ounces) evaporated milk (about ⅔ cup)**

¼   **cup (½ stick) butter or margarine**

2   **cups (12-ounce package) HERSHEY'S SPECIAL DARK Chocolate Chips**

1   **cup MAUNA LOA Macadamia Nut Baking Pieces**

½   **teaspoon vanilla extract**

1. Line 8- or 9-inch square pan with foil, extending foil over edges of pan.

2. Combine sugar, marshmallow creme, evaporated milk and butter in heavy medium saucepan. Cook over medium heat, stirring constantly, to a full boil. Boil, stirring constantly, 5 minutes.

3. Remove from heat; add chocolate chips. Stir just until chips are melted. Stir in nuts and vanilla; pour into prepared pan.

4. Refrigerate 1 hour or until firm. Lift fudge out of pan using foil; place on cutting board. Cut into squares. Store tightly covered in a cool, dry place.

No-Bake Chocolate Cake Roll

makes about 12 servings

1   package (4-serving size) vanilla instant pudding and pie filling mix

3   tablespoons HERSHEY'S Cocoa, divided

1   cup milk

1   container (8 ounces) frozen non-dairy whipped topping, thawed and divided

1   package (9 ounces) crisp chocolate wafers

    HERSHEY'S HUGSBRAND Candies and HERSHEY'S KISSESBRAND Milk Chocolates

1. Combine pudding mix and 2 tablespoons cocoa in small bowl. Add milk; beat on low speed of mixer until smooth and thickened. Fold in 1 cup whipped topping, blending well.

2. Spread about 1 tablespoon pudding mixture onto top of each chocolate wafer; put wafers together in stacks of 4 or 5. On foil, stand wafers on edge to make one long roll. Wrap tightly; refrigerate 5 to 6 hours.

3. Sift remaining 1 tablespoon cocoa over remaining 2½ cups whipped topping; blend well. Unwrap roll; place on serving tray. Spread whipped topping mixture over entire roll. Remove wrappers from candies; place on roll to garnish. To serve, slice diagonally at 45° angle. Cover; refrigerate leftover dessert.

Chocolate Peanut Clusters

makes about 2 dozen candies

½ cup **HERSHEY'S Milk Chocolate Chips**

½ cup **HERSHEY'S SPECIAL DARK Chocolate Chips or HERSHEY'S Semi-Sweet Chocolate Chips**

1 **tablespoon shortening (do not use butter, margarine, spread or oil)**

1 **cup unsalted, roasted peanuts**

1. Place milk chocolate chips, SPECIAL DARK chocolate chips and shortening in small microwave-safe bowl. Microwave at MEDIUM (50%) 1 to 1½ minutes or just until chips are melted and mixture is smooth when stirred. Stir in peanuts.

2. Drop by teaspoons into 1-inch diameter candy or petit four papers. Refrigerate until firm, about 1 hour. Store in airtight container in cool, dry place.

no-bake treats

Two Great Tastes Pudding Parfaits

makes 4 to 6 servings

1   package (6-serving size) vanilla
    cook & serve pudding and pie
    filling mix*

3½ cups milk

1   cup REESE'S Peanut Butter Chips

1   cup HERSHEY'S MINI KISSESBRAND
    Milk Chocolates

    Whipped topping (optional)

    Additional MINI KISSESBRAND Milk
    Chocolates or grated chocolate

*Do not use instant pudding mix.

1. Combine pudding mix and 3½ cups milk in large heavy saucepan (rather than amount listed in package directions). Cook over medium heat, stirring constantly, until mixture comes to a full boil. Remove from heat; divide hot mixture between 2 heatproof medium bowls.

2. Immediately stir peanut butter chips into mixture in one bowl and chocolates into second bowl. Stir both mixtures until chips are melted and mixture is smooth. Cool slightly, stirring occasionally.

3. Alternately layer peanut butter and chocolate mixtures in parfait dishes, wine glasses or dessert dishes. Place plastic wrap directly onto surface of each dessert; refrigerate about 6 hours. Garnish with whipped topping, if desired, and chocolate pieces.

SPECIAL DARK® Fudge Fondue

makes 1½ cups

2   cups (12-ounce package) **HERSHEY'S SPECIAL DARK Chocolate Chips**

½   cup light cream

2   teaspoons vanilla extract

Assorted fondue dippers such as marshmallows, cherries, grapes, mandarin orange segments, pineapple chunks, strawberries, slices of other fresh fruits, small pieces of cake or small brownies

1. Place chocolate chips and light cream in medium microwave-safe bowl. Microwave at MEDIUM (50%) 1 minute or just until chips are melted and mixture is smooth when stirred. Stir in vanilla.

2. Pour into fondue pot or chafing dish; serve warm with fondue dippers. If mixture thickens, stir in additional light cream, one tablespoon at a time. Refrigerate leftover fondue.

Stovetop Directions: Combine chocolate chips and light cream in heavy medium saucepan. Cook over low heat, stirring constantly, until chips are melted and mixture is hot. Stir in vanilla and continue as in Step 2 above.

no-bake treats

Chocolate Cup Brownie Sundae

makes 6 cups

6 **CHOCOLATE SHELLS (recipe follows)**

Brownie pieces

Ice cream (any flavor)

HERSHEY'S Syrup

Strawberries, raspberries, blueberries or other fresh fruit slices

Whipped topping or sweetened whipped cream

1. At least 2 hours in advance, prepare CHOCOLATE SHELLS.

2. For each sundae, remove foil from outside of chocolate shell. Place brownie pieces in bottom of chocolate shell. Top with ice cream. Garnish with syrup, fresh fruit and whipped topping.

Chocolate Shells:

Line 6 muffin cups (2½ inches in diameter) with foil or paper baking cups. Place 24 unwrapped HERSHEY'S KISSESBRAND Milk Chocolates (or ⅔ cup HERSHEY'S MINI KISSESBRAND Milk Chocolates) or HERSHEY'S KISSESBRAND SPECIAL DARK Mildly Sweet Chocolates in medium microwave-safe bowl. Microwave at MEDIUM (50%) 1 minute; stir. If necessary, microwave at MEDIUM an additional 15 seconds at a time, stirring after each heating, until chocolates are melted and smooth when stirred. Cool slightly.

Coat inside of pleated surfaces and bottom of bake cups thickly and evenly with melted chocolate using a soft-bristled pastry brush. Refrigerate coated cups 10 minutes or until set; recoat any thin spots with melted chocolate. (If necessary, reheat chocolate at MEDIUM for a few seconds.) Refrigerate cups until very firm, 2 hours or overnight. Cover; refrigerate until ready to use.

no-bake treats

Chocolate Dipped Fruit

makes about ½ cup coating

1   cup **HERSHEY'S SPECIAL DARK Chocolate Chips or HERSHEY'S Semi-Sweet Chocolate Chips**

1   **tablespoon shortening (do not use butter, margarine, spread or oil)**

Assorted fresh fruit, washed and chilled

1. Combine chocolate chips and shortening in heavy saucepan. Cook over very low heat, stirring constantly, until chips are melted. Remove from heat; cool slightly.

2. Dip fruit or fruit slices about ⅔ of the way into chocolate mixture. Shake gently to remove excess chocolate.

3. Place on wax paper-covered tray. Refrigerate, uncovered, until chocolate is firm, about 30 minutes.

Microwave Instructions: Place chocolate chips and shortening in small microwave-safe bowl. Microwave at MEDIUM (50%) 1 to 1½ minutes or just until chips are melted and mixture is smooth when stirred. Allow to cool slightly. Dip and serve fruit as directed above.

no-bake treats

REESE'S® Haystacks

makes about 2 dozen treats

1⅔ **cups (10-ounce package) REESE'S Peanut Butter Chips**

1 **tablespoon shortening (do not use butter, margarine, spread or oil)**

2½ **cups (5-ounce can) chow mein noodles**

1. Line tray with wax paper.

2. Place peanut butter chips and shortening in medium microwave-safe bowl. Microwave at MEDIUM (50%) 1 minute; stir. If necessary, microwave at MEDIUM an additional 15 seconds at a time, stirring after each heating, just until chips are melted and mixture is smooth when stirred. Immediately add chow mein noodles; stir to coat.

3. Drop mixture by heaping teaspoons onto prepared tray or into paper candy cups. Let stand until firm. If necessary, cover and refrigerate several minutes until firm. Store in tightly covered container.

Drink *it up*

Choco-Berry Cooler

makes 1 (14-ounce) serving

¾   **cup cold milk**

¼   **cup sliced fresh strawberries**

2   **tablespoons HERSHEY'S Syrup**

2   **tablespoons plus 2 small scoops vanilla ice cream, divided**

     Cold ginger ale or club soda

     Fresh strawberry and mint leaves (optional)

1. Place milk, strawberries, chocolate syrup and 2 tablespoons ice cream in blender container. Cover and blend until smooth.

2. Alternate remaining 2 scoops of ice cream and chocolate mixture in tall ice cream soda glass; fill glass with ginger ale. Garnish with a fresh strawberry and mint leaves, if desired. Serve immediately.

Variations: Before blending, substitute one of the following fruits for fresh strawberries:
• 3 tablespoons frozen strawberries with syrup, thawed
• ½ peeled fresh peach or ⅓ cup canned peach slices
• 2 slices canned pineapple or ¼ cup canned crushed pineapple
• ¼ cup sweetened fresh raspberries or 3 tablespoons frozen raspberries with syrup, thawed

Double Strawberry Milkshake

makes about 1 (10-ounce) serving

2   to 3 scoops (about 1 cup) strawberry ice cream or frozen yogurt

½   cup cold milk

3   tablespoons HERSHEY'S Strawberry Syrup

    Whipped topping (optional)

    Strawberry (optional)

1. Place ice cream, milk and strawberry syrup in blender container. Cover; blend until smooth.

2. Garnish with whipped topping and strawberry, if desired.

drink it up

Chocolate Peanut Butter Milkshake

makes 2 (10-ounce) servings

1½ cups vanilla ice cream

1 cup cold milk

⅓ cup HERSHEY'S Syrup

2 tablespoons REESE'S Peanut Butter Topping or REESE'S Creamy Peanut Butter

Whipped topping

Maraschino cherry (optional)

1. Place ice cream, milk, chocolate syrup and topping in blender container. Cover; blend until smooth.

2. Garnish with whipped topping and cherry, if desired.

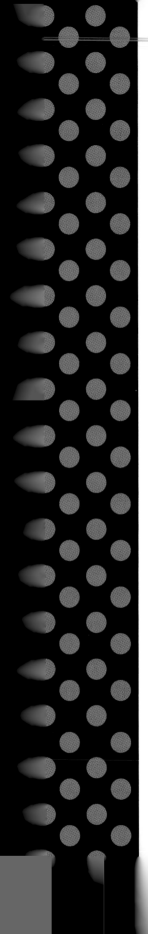

Classic Caramel Milkshake

makes 2 large (12-ounce) servings

1	cup cold milk
⅓	cup **HERSHEY'S Caramel Syrup** or **HERSHEY'S Classic Caramel Sundae Syrup**
2	cups vanilla ice cream

Place milk, caramel syrup and ice cream in blender container. Cover; blend until smooth and thick. Serve immediately.

drink it up

Chocolate Cherry Milkshake

makes 2 (10-ounce) servings

4   scoops (about 2 cups) vanilla ice cream or frozen yogurt

¾   cup cold milk

¼   cup HERSHEY'S Syrup

8   maraschino cherries, stems removed

     Whipped topping and additional cherries (optional)

1. Place ice cream, milk, chocolate syrup and cherries in blender container. Cover; blend until smooth.

2. Garnish with whipped topping and additional cherries, if desired.

Strawberry Pink Lemonade

makes about 4 servings or 1 quart lemonade

1   **can (6 ounces) frozen lemonade concentrate, partially thawed**

2⅔   **cups cold water**

⅓   **cup HERSHEY'S Strawberry Syrup**

Stir together lemonade concentrate, water and strawberry syrup in pitcher. Serve in tall glasses over crushed ice.

Strawberry Pink Lemonade Ice Pops: Stir together lemonade concentrate, water and strawberry syrup as directed above. Divide mixture among 8 paper cold drink cups (5 ounces each). Freeze about 1 hour; insert wooden popsicle sticks into strawberry mixture. Cover; freeze until firm. Peel off cups to serve. Makes 8 pops.

Single Serving: Place about 1½ tablespoons strawberry syrup in bottom of tall glass. Fill with ice. Pour lemonade over ice. Stir to blend or serve with long spoon for blending.

drink it up

Peachy Chocolate Yogurt Smoothie

makes 4 servings

⅔   **cup peeled fresh peach slices or 1 package (10 ounces) frozen peach slices, thawed and drained**

½   **teaspoon vanilla or almond extract**

2   **cups (1 pint) vanilla nonfat frozen yogurt**

¼   **cup HERSHEY'S Syrup**

¼   **cup nonfat milk**

1. Place peaches and vanilla extract in blender container. Cover; blend until smooth.

2. Add frozen yogurt, chocolate syrup and milk. Cover; blend until smooth. Serve immediately.

drink it up

Peanut Butter & Jelly Spin

makes 1 serving

2   tablespoons REESE'S Creamy Peanut Butter

2   tablespoons jelly or jam (grape, raspberry or strawberry)

½   cup milk

1   cup vanilla ice cream

Combine peanut butter and jelly. Place in blender container. Add milk and ice cream. Cover; blend until smooth. Pour into tall glass. Serve immediately.

"Perfectly Chocolate" Hot Cocoa

makes 1 serving

2	tablespoons sugar
2	to 3 teaspoons HERSHEY'S Cocoa
	Dash salt
1	cup milk
¼	teaspoon vanilla extract

Mix sugar, cocoa and salt in large mug. Heat milk in microwave at HIGH (100%) 1½ minutes or until hot. Gradually add hot milk to cocoa mixture in mug, stirring until well blended. Stir in vanilla.

Rich and Adult: Increase cocoa to 2 tablespoons; follow recipe above.

Lower Fat: Use nonfat milk; follow recipe above.

Sugar Free: Omit sugar. Combine cocoa and salt in mug. Proceed as above, using nonfat milk. Stir in vanilla and sugar substitute with sweetening equivalence of 2 tablespoons sugar.

drink it up

Drinking Chocolate

makes 2 servings

2   sections (½ ounce each)
      HERSHEY'S Unsweetened
      Chocolate Baking Bar
2   tablespoons hot water
¼   cup sugar
      Dash of salt
¼   cup milk, warmed
¼   teaspoon vanilla extract

Place chocolate and water in top of small double boiler. Melt over simmering water, stirring until smooth. Stir in sugar and salt, blending thoroughly. Gradually blend in warm milk. Heat, stirring occasionally, until hot. Stir in vanilla. Pour into demitasse cups. Garnish as desired. Serve immediately.

drink it up

Hot Cocoa Mocha

makes 3 to 4 servings

¼   **cup sugar**

2   **tablespoons HERSHEY'S Cocoa**

2   **tablespoons water**

1   **cup whipping cream**

1¼   **to 2 cups hot coffee**

1. Stir together sugar and cocoa in microwave-safe 2-cup measure. Add water; stir until well blended. Microwave at HIGH (100%) 30 to 45 seconds or until mixture boils.

2. Add whipping cream; stir until well blended. Microwave at HIGH 1 to 1½ minutes or until hot. Combine cocoa mixture and coffee. Serve immediately.

celebrate the Holidays

Holiday Cookies on a Stick

makes about 18 (3½-inch) cookies

1	cup (2 sticks) butter or margarine, softened
¾	cup granulated sugar
¾	cup packed light brown sugar
1	teaspoon vanilla extract
2	eggs
2⅓	cups all-purpose flour
½	cup HERSHEY'S Cocoa
1	teaspoon baking soda
½	teaspoon salt
	About 18 wooden ice cream sticks
1	container (16 ounces) vanilla ready-to-spread frosting (optional)
	Decorating icing in tube, colored sugar, candy sprinkles, HERSHEY'S MINI KISSESBRAND Milk Chocolates

1. Heat oven to 350°F.

2. Beat butter, granulated sugar, brown sugar and vanilla in large bowl on medium speed of mixer until creamy. Add eggs; beat well. Stir together flour, cocoa, baking soda and salt; gradually add to butter mixture, beating until well blended.

3. Drop dough by scant ¼ cupfuls onto ungreased cookie sheet, about 3 inches apart. Shape into balls. Insert wooden stick about three-fourths of the way into side of each ball. Flatten slightly.

4. Bake 8 to 10 minutes or until set. (Cookies will spread during baking.) Cool 3 minutes; using wide spatula, carefully remove from cookie sheet to wire rack. Cool completely.

5. Spread with frosting, if desired. Decorate as desired with holiday motifs, such as a star, tree, candy cane, holly and Santa using decorating icing and garnishes.

celebrate the holidays

Yummy Mummy Cookies

makes about 30 cookies

⅔ cup butter or margarine, softened

1 cup sugar

2 teaspoons vanilla extract

2 eggs

2½ cups all-purpose flour

½ cup HERSHEY'S Cocoa

½ teaspoon salt

¼ teaspoon baking soda

1 cup HERSHEY'S Mini Chips Semi-Sweet Chocolate

1 to 2 packages (12 ounces each) HERSHEY'S Premier White Chips

1 to 2 tablespoons shortening (do not use butter, margarine, spread or oil)

Additional HERSHEY'S Mini Chips Semi-Sweet Chocolate

1. Beat butter, sugar and vanilla in large bowl until creamy. Add eggs; beat well. Stir together flour, cocoa, salt and baking soda; gradually add to butter mixture, beating until blended. Stir in 1 cup small chocolate chips. Refrigerate dough 15 to 20 minutes or until firm enough to handle.

2. Heat oven to 350°F.

3. To form body, using 1 tablespoon dough, roll into 3½-inch carrot shape; place on ungreased cookie sheet. To form head, using 1 teaspoon dough, roll into ball the size and shape of a grape; press onto wide end of body. Repeat with remaining dough.

4. Bake 8 to 9 minutes or until set. Cool slightly; remove from cookie sheet to wire rack. Cool completely.

5. Place 2 cups (12-ounce package) white chips and 1 tablespoon shortening in microwave-safe pie plate or shallow bowl. Microwave at MEDIUM (50%) 1 minute; stir until chips are melted.

6. Coat tops of cookies by placing one cookie at a time on table knife or narrow metal spatula; spoon white chip mixture evenly over cookie to coat. (If mixture begins to thicken, return to microwave for a few seconds). Place coated cookies on wax paper. Melt additional chips with shortening, if needed, for additional coating. As coating begins to set on cookies, using a toothpick, score lines and facial features into coating to resemble mummy. Place 2 small chocolate chips on each cookie for eyes. Store, covered, in cool, dry place.

Jack-O-Lantern Brownie

makes 12 to 16 servings

¾ cup (1½ sticks) butter or margarine, melted

1½ cups sugar

1½ teaspoons vanilla extract

3 eggs

¾ cup all-purpose flour

½ cup HERSHEY'S Cocoa

½ teaspoon baking powder

¼ teaspoon salt

Yellow and red food color

1 can (16 ounces) vanilla frosting

Suggested garnishes: HERSHEY'S MINI KISSESBRAND Milk Chocolates, assorted candies as TWIZZLERS NIBS Licorice Bits, TWIZZLERS PULL-N-PEEL, HEATH English Toffee Bits

1. Heat oven to 350°F. Grease 12-inch round pizza pan. If using a disposable pan, place on baking sheet to bake.

2. Beat melted butter, sugar and vanilla with spoon in large bowl. Beat in eggs. Stir in dry ingredients; beat with spoon until well blended. Spread in pan.

3. Bake 20 to 22 minutes or until top springs back when touched lightly in center. Cool completely. Add yellow and red food color to frosting for desired shade of orange. Frost brownie; garnish to resemble a jack-o-lantern.

Sweetheart Layer Bars

makes 24 to 36 bars

1	cup (2 sticks) butter or margarine, divided
1½	cups finely crushed unsalted thin pretzels or pretzel sticks
1	cup HERSHEY'S MINI KISSESBRAND Milk Chocolates
1	can (14 ounces) sweetened condensed milk (not evaporated milk)
¾	cup HERSHEY'S Cocoa
2	cups MOUNDS Sweetened Coconut Flakes, tinted*

To tint coconut: Place 1 teaspoon water and ½ teaspoon red food color in small bowl; stir in 2 cups coconut flakes. With fork, toss until evenly coated.

1. Heat oven to 350°F.

2. Place ¾ cup butter (1½ sticks) in 13×9×2-inch baking pan; place in oven just until butter melts. Remove from oven. Stir in crushed pretzels; press evenly onto bottom of pan. Sprinkle chocolates over pretzel layer.

3. Place sweetened condensed milk, cocoa and remaining ¼ cup butter (½ stick) in small microwave-safe bowl. Microwave at MEDIUM (50%) 1 to 1½ minutes or until mixture is melted and smooth when stirred; carefully pour over chocolate layer in pan. Top with coconut; press firmly down onto chocolate layer.

4. Bake 25 to 30 minutes or until lightly browned around edges. Cool completely in pan on wire rack. Cut into heart-shaped pieces with cookie cutters or cut into bars.

celebrate the holidays

Jolly Peanut Butter Gingerbread Cookies

makes about 6 dozen cookies

1⅔ cups (10-ounce package) REESE'S Peanut Butter Chips

¾ cup (1½ sticks) butter or margarine, softened

1 cup packed light brown sugar

1 cup dark corn syrup

2 eggs

5 cups all-purpose flour

1 teaspoon baking soda

½ teaspoon ground cinnamon

¼ teaspoon ground ginger

¼ teaspoon salt

1. Place peanut butter chips in small microwave-safe bowl. Microwave at MEDIUM (50%) 1 minute; stir. If necessary, microwave at MEDIUM an additional 15 seconds at a time, stirring after each heating, until chips are melted when stirred. Beat melted peanut butter chips and butter in large bowl until well blended. Add brown sugar, corn syrup and eggs; beat until fluffy.

2. Stir together flour, baking soda, cinnamon, ginger and salt. Add half of flour mixture to butter mixture; beat on low speed of mixer until smooth. With wooden spoon, stir in remaining flour mixture until well blended. Divide into thirds; wrap each in plastic wrap. Refrigerate at least 1 hour or until dough is firm enough to roll.

3. Heat oven to 325°F. On lightly floured surface, roll 1 dough portion at a time to ⅛-inch thickness; cut into holiday shapes with floured cookie cutters. Place on ungreased cookie sheet.

4. Bake 10 to 12 minutes or until set and lightly browned. Cool slightly; remove from cookie sheet to wire rack. Cool completely. Frost and decorate as desired.

celebrate the holidays

KISSES® Candy Holiday Twists

make as desired

HERSHEY'S KISSESBRAND **Milk Chocolates**

1 **bag small pretzels (twisted)**

HERSHEY'S HERSHEY-ETS **Candy Coated Milk Chocolates in red and green colors**

Additional decorative garnishes such as: small holiday themed candies, nut pieces, miniature marshmallows, candied cherry pieces

1. Heat oven to 350°F. Remove wrappers from chocolates.

2. Place pretzels on ungreased cookie sheet. Place 1 unwrapped chocolate on top of each pretzel.

3. Bake 2 to 3 minutes or until the chocolate starts to soften, but is not melting. (Do not overheat. Melted chocolate retains its shape until disturbed. Heat only until you can gently push chocolate tip down.)

4. Remove from oven; gently press small chocolates and other decorative garnishes on top of the soft chocolate piece. Cool and serve.

celebrate the holidays

Pinecone Cookies

makes about 48 cookies

6 tablespoons butter or margarine

⅓ cup HERSHEY'S Cocoa or HERSHEY'S SPECIAL DARK Cocoa

1 cup sugar

2 eggs

1 teaspoon vanilla extract

2 cups all-purpose flour

½ teaspoon baking powder

½ teaspoon salt

¼ teaspoon baking soda

Light corn syrup

Sliced almonds

1. Melt butter in small saucepan; remove from heat. Add cocoa; blend well. Beat sugar, eggs and vanilla in large bowl; blend in cocoa mixture. Stir together flour, baking powder, salt and baking soda; add to cocoa mixture, beating until smooth. Refrigerate dough about 1 hour or until firm enough to roll.

2. Heat oven to 350°F. Lightly grease cookie sheet or line with parchment paper. Roll small portion of dough between two pieces of wax paper to ⅛-inch thickness. Cut into pinecone shapes using 2- or 2½-inch oval cookie cutter. Place on prepared cookie sheet; lightly brush cookies with corn syrup. Arrange almonds in pinecone fashion; lightly drizzle or brush almonds with corn syrup. Repeat with remaining dough.

3. Bake 7 to 8 minutes or until set. Remove from cookie sheet to wire rack; cool completely.

Eerie Eyeball Cookies

makes about 48 cookies

½	cup shortening
¾	cup REESE'S Creamy Peanut Butter
⅓	cup granulated sugar
⅓	cup packed light brown sugar
1	egg
2	tablespoons milk
1	teaspoon vanilla extract
1½	cups all-purpose flour
1	teaspoon baking soda
½	teaspoon salt
	Additional granulated sugar
	About 1 cup vanilla frosting (homemade or ready-to- spread)
	Red and black decorator frosting in tubes
	WHOPPERS Malted Milk Balls

1. Heat oven to 375°F. Beat shortening and peanut butter in large bowl until well blended. Add ⅓ cup granulated sugar and brown sugar; beat until fluffy. Add egg, milk and vanilla; beat well. Stir together flour, baking soda and salt; gradually beat into peanut butter mixture.

2. Shape dough into 1-inch balls. Roll in additional granulated sugar; place on ungreased cookie sheet.

3. Bake 8 to 10 minutes or until lightly browned. Remove from cookie sheet to wire rack. Cool completely.

4. Frost center of cookie with vanilla frosting to form white portion of eye. Decorate with red and black frostings to form outline of eye and bloodshot markings. Press malted milk ball "iris" into center of eye.

celebrate the holidays

Valentine Sugar Cookie Pops

makes about 12 cookies

¾ cup (1½ sticks) butter or margarine, softened
¾ cup sugar
1 egg
½ teaspoon vanilla extract
1¾ cups all-purpose flour
½ teaspoon baking soda
¼ teaspoon salt
12 wooden ice cream sticks
    CHOCOLATE DRIZZLE (recipe follows)
    Assorted frostings, sugars and small candies

1. Heat oven to 350°F. Beat butter and sugar in medium bowl until creamy. Add egg and vanilla; beat well. Stir together flour, baking soda and salt; gradually add to butter mixture, beating until blended. (If necessary, refrigerate dough until firm enough to handle.)

2. Roll ¼ cup dough into ball; place on ungreased cookie sheet, 3 cookies per sheet. (Cookies spread while baking.) Insert wooden stick about three-quarters of the way into side of each ball. Flatten slightly.

3. Bake 13 to 15 minutes or until outside edges are lightly browned and center is set. Cool several minutes on cookie sheet; remove to wire rack. Cool completely.

4. Decorate with CHOCOLATE DRIZZLE and assorted frostings, sugars and small candies to make Valentine cookies.

Chocolate Drizzle: Place ½ cup HERSHEY'S SPECIAL DARK Chocolate Chips or HERSHEY'S Semi-Sweet Chocolate Chips and 1 teaspoon shortening (do not use butter, margarine, spread or oil) in small microwave-safe bowl. Microwave at MEDIUM (50%) 30 seconds; stir. If necessary, microwave at MEDIUM an additional 10 seconds at a time, stirring after each heating, until chocolate is melted when stirred.

Easy Easter KISSES® & Peanut Butter Cup Pie

makes 8 servings

16	REESE'S Peanut Butter Cups Miniatures, unwrapped and chopped
5¼	cups (12 ounces) frozen non-dairy whipped topping, thawed and divided
2	tablespoons REESE'S Creamy Peanut Butter
1	prepared (6-ounce) graham cracker crumb crust
27	HERSHEY'S KISSESᴮᴿᴬᴺᴰ Milk Chocolates, unwrapped
24	REESE'S Peanut Butter Cups Miniatures or HERSHEY'S KISSESᴮᴿᴬᴺᴰ Milk Chocolates, unwrapped
24	HERSHEY'S Candy-Coated Milk Chocolate Eggs

1. Combine chopped peanut butter cups, 2 cups whipped topping and peanut butter in large bowl. Spread onto bottom of crumb crust.

2. Place 27 milk chocolate pieces in small microwave-safe bowl. Microwave at MEDIUM (50%) 1 minute; stir. If necessary, microwave at MEDIUM an additional 15 seconds at a time, stirring after each heating, until chocolate is melted and smooth when stirred. Stir in 2 cups whipped topping; spread on top of peanut butter layer. Cover; refrigerate until firm.

3. Spread remaining 1¼ cups whipped topping on top of pie. Cut into slices and decorate each slice with 3 candies and 3 candy eggs. Serve immediately; refrigerate leftovers.

celebrate the holidays

KISSES® Sweetheart Cookies

yield will vary according to cookie recipe used

Sugar Cookie Dough (purchased or your favorite recipe)

HERSHEY'S Cocoa

48   HERSHEY'S KISSESBRAND Milk Chocolates, unwrapped*

1   teaspoon shortening (do not use butter, margarine, spread or oil)

Forty-eight KISSESBRAND Milk Chocolates is enough to garnish about 3 dozen cookies following these directions; adjust as necessary for sugar cookie recipe.

1. Heat oven as directed for sugar cookies. Divide dough in half; roll out one half at a time to ¼-inch thickness following package or recipe directions. Cut out with 2-inch heart shaped cookie cutters; place on ungreased cookie sheet.

2. Bake according to package or recipe directions. Cool completely on cooling racks. Sprinkle cookies with cocoa.

3. Place 12 chocolates and shortening in small microwave-safe bowl. Microwave at MEDIUM (50%) 1 minute; stir. If necessary, microwave at MEDIUM 15 seconds at a time, stirring after each heating, until chocolates are melted and mixture is smooth when stirred. Drizzle onto cookies. Before drizzle sets, place 1 chocolate in center of each heart.

celebrate the holidays

Christmas Cupcakes

makes about 33 cupcakes

2   cups sugar

1¾   cups all-purpose flour

¾   cup HERSHEY'S Cocoa or HERSHEY'S SPECIAL DARK Cocoa

1½   teaspoons baking powder

1½   teaspoons baking soda

1   teaspoon salt

2   eggs

1   cup milk

½   cup vegetable oil

2   teaspoons vanilla extract

1   cup boiling water

1   can (16 ounces) creamy vanilla ready-to-spread frosting

     MOUNDS Sweetened Coconut Flakes

     Assorted candies such as candy canes, spearmint leaves and TWIZZLERS Strawberry Twists

1. Heat oven to 350°F. Line muffin cups (2½ inches in diameter) with paper or foil bake cups.

2. Stir together sugar, flour, cocoa, baking powder, baking soda and salt in large bowl. Add eggs, milk, oil and vanilla; beat on medium speed of electric mixer 2 minutes. Stir in boiling water (batter will be thin). Fill muffin cups ⅔ full with batter.

3. Bake 22 to 25 minutes or until wooden pick inserted in center comes out clean. Cool completely.

4. Frost each cupcake with vanilla frosting. Decorate with coconut and candies in various Christmas themes. (For example, slice spearmint leaves and place on cupcake surface along with slices of strawberry twists to resemble holly leaves and berries.)

Easter Nest Cookies

makes about 42 cookies

1½	cups all-purpose flour
1	teaspoon baking powder
½	teaspoon salt
¾	cup (1½ sticks) butter
2	cups miniature marshmallows
½	cup sugar
1	egg white
1	teaspoon vanilla extract
½	teaspoon almond extract
3¾	cups MOUNDS Sweetened Coconut Flakes, divided
	JOLLY RANCHER Jelly Beans
	HERSHEY'S Candy Coated Milk Chocolate Eggs

1. Heat oven to 375°F.

2. Stir together flour, baking powder and salt; set aside. Place butter and marshmallows in microwave-safe bowl. Microwave at HIGH (100%) 1 to 1½ minutes or just until mixture melts when stirred. Beat sugar, egg white, vanilla and almond extract in separate bowl; add melted butter mixture, beating until light and fluffy. Gradually add flour mixture, beating until blended. Stir in 2 cups coconut.

3. Shape dough into 1-inch balls; roll balls in remaining 1¾ cups coconut, tinting coconut, if desired.* Place balls on ungreased cookie sheet. Press thumb into center of each ball, creating shallow depression.

4. Bake 8 to 10 minutes or just until lightly browned. Place 1 to 3 jelly beans and milk chocolate eggs in center of each cookie. Transfer to wire rack; cool completely.

To tint coconut: Place ¾ teaspoon water and a few drops food color in small bowl; stir in 1¾ cups coconut. Toss with fork until evenly tinted; cover.

Halloween Cookies on a Stick

makes about 18 (3½-inch) cookies

1	cup (2 sticks) butter or margarine, softened
¾	cup granulated sugar
¾	cup packed light brown sugar
1	teaspoon vanilla extract
2	eggs
2½	cups all-purpose flour
⅓	cup HERSHEY'S Cocoa
1	teaspoon baking soda
½	teaspoon salt
	About 18 wooden ice cream sticks
	Decorating icing

1. Heat oven to 350°F. Beat butter, granulated sugar, brown sugar and vanilla in large bowl on medium speed of mixer until creamy. Add eggs; beat well. Stir together flour, cocoa, baking soda and salt; gradually add to butter mixture, beating until well blended.

2. Drop dough by scant ¼ cupfuls onto ungreased cookie sheet, about 3 inches apart. Shape into balls. Insert wooden stick about halfway into center of each. Flatten slightly.

3. Bake 10 to 12 minutes or until set. Cool 3 minutes; carefully remove from cookie sheet to wire rack. Cool completely.

4. Decorate as desired with decorating icing.

Mini-KISSed Shamrock Cookies

makes about 30 cookies

1 pouch (1 pound 1.5 ounces) sugar cookie mix

⅔ cup HERSHEY'S Cocoa

⅓ cup vegetable oil

2 eggs, slightly beaten

1 tablespoon plus 1 teaspoon water

SHAMROCK FROSTING (recipe follows)

HERSHEY'S MINI KISSESBRAND Milk Chocolates

Shamrock Frosting

1 tablespoon butter or margarine, softened

1 cup powdered sugar

1 tablespoon hot milk or light cream

½ teaspoon vanilla extract

2 or 3 drops green food color

Mix all ingredients until smooth.

1. Heat oven to 350°F. Combine cookie mix and cocoa in large bowl; stir. Add oil, eggs and water; mix with spoon or fork until well combined. Dough will clump together and be easy to handle.

2. Shape dough into balls, using about 1 level measuring teaspoon dough for each ball. Cluster 3 balls on ungreased cookie sheet to form shamrock; flatten each "leaf" slightly. Shape 1 ball into pencil shape for stem; tuck stem under bottom of shamrock "leaves."

3. Bake 7 to 8 minutes or until set. Cool slightly; remove from cookie sheet to wire rack. Cool completely.

4. Outline shamrock and stem with SHAMROCK FROSTING. Place small amount of frosting in center of each cookie. Press chocolate piece in center.

celebrate the holidays

HERSHEY'S® Firecracker Cake

makes 8 to 10 servings

4   eggs, separated

½   cup plus ⅓ cup granulated sugar, divided

1   teaspoon vanilla extract

½   cup all-purpose flour

⅓   cup HERSHEY'S Cocoa

¼   teaspoon baking powder

¼   teaspoon baking soda

⅛   teaspoon salt

⅓   cup water

   Powdered sugar

1   cup cherry pie filling

1   tub (8 ounces) frozen whipped topping, thawed and divided

   HERSHEY'S KISSESBRAND Milk Chocolates, HERSHEY'S HUGSBRAND Candies, HERSHEY'S MINIATURES Chocolate Bars

   Blueberries, raspberries, halved strawberries

1   TWIZZLERS Strawberry Twists

1. Heat oven to 375°F. Line 15½×10-½×1-inch jelly-roll pan with foil; generously grease foil.

2. Beat egg whites in large bowl until foamy; gradually add ½ cup granulated sugar, beating until stiff peaks form.

3. Beat egg yolks and vanilla in small bowl on high speed of mixer about 3 minutes. Gradually add remaining ⅓ cup granulated sugar; continue beating 2 minutes. Combine flour, cocoa, baking powder, baking soda and salt; add to egg yolk mixture alternately with water on low speed, beating just until batter is smooth.

4. Fold chocolate mixture gradually into egg whites; spread evenly in prepared pan.

5. Bake 12 to 15 minutes or until top springs back when touched lightly in center. Immediately loosen cake from edges of pan; invert on towel sprinkled with powdered sugar. Carefully remove foil. Immediately roll cake in towel, starting from narrow end; place on wire rack to cool.

6. Unroll cake; remove towel. Spread with pie filling and 1½ cups whipped topping; reroll cake. Frost cake with remaining whipped topping. Place candies and fruit on frosted cake so that they form stripes around the cake. Add strawberry twist for "wick." Refrigerate until serving time.

Patriotic Cocoa Cupcakes

makes about 30 cupcakes

2 cups sugar
1¾ cups all-purpose flour
¾ cup HERSHEY'S Cocoa
2 teaspoons baking soda
1 teaspoon baking powder
1 teaspoon salt
2 eggs
1 cup buttermilk or sour milk*
1 cup boiling water
½ cup vegetable oil
1 teaspoon vanilla extract
VANILLA FROSTING (recipe follows)
Chocolate stars or blue and red decorating icings (in tube)

*To sour milk: Use 1 tablespoon white vinegar plus milk to equal 1 cup.

1. Heat oven to 350°F. Grease and flour muffin cups (2½ inches in diameter) or line with paper bake cups.

2. Combine dry ingredients in large bowl. Add eggs, buttermilk, water, oil and vanilla; beat on medium speed of mixer 2 minutes (batter will be thin). Fill cups ⅔ full with batter.

3. Bake 15 minutes or until wooden pick inserted in centers comes out clean. Remove cupcakes from pan. Cool completely. To make chocolate stars for garnish, if desired, cut several cupcakes into ½-inch slices; cut out star shapes from cake slices. Frost remaining cupcakes with VANILLA FROSTING. Garnish with chocolate stars or with blue and red decorating icing.

Vanilla Frosting: Beat ¼ cup (½ stick) softened butter, ¼ cup shortening and 2 teaspoons vanilla extract in large bowl. Add 1 cup powdered sugar; beat until creamy. Add 3 cups powdered sugar alternately with 3 to 4 tablespoons milk, beating to spreading consistency. Makes about 2⅓ cups frosting.

celebrate the holidays

creative Crafts

HERSHEY'S® Pinwheel Party Favors

MATERIALS:

- Scissors
- Construction paper/double-sided scrapbook paper
- Ruler
- Pencil
- Glue (low-temperature glue gun and glue sticks, non-toxic craft glue, glue stick or safe confectioners' glue)*
- HERSHEY'S KISSESBRAND Chocolates
- 6-inch lengths of 12-gauge floral wire
- Straws

Use hot melt glue with adult supervision. Safe confectioners' glue recipe on page 112.

INSTRUCTIONS:

1. Cut a 6-inch square out of the construction paper.

2. Place a ruler diagonally, corner to corner and draw a line with the pencil. Repeat with the other 2 corners.

3. Cut each line beginning at the outside corner and ending within an inch of the center of the square.

4. One at a time, fold each corner to the center of the square and glue. When all 4 corners are glued, you have formed the pinwheel.

5. Glue the flat side of 1 chocolate to the center of the pinwheel.

6. Insert 1 end of the floral wire through the back center of the pinwheel into the chocolate.

7. Slip the straw over the remaining length of the floral wire.

8. Holding onto only the straw, blow gently on the pinwheel and watch it spin.

Note: Completed craft is for decorative purpose only. Candy should not be eaten.

HERSHEY'S® HUGS® & KISSES®
Sweetheart Roses

MATERIALS:

- Glue (low-temperature glue gun and glue sticks, non-toxic craft glue, glue stick or safe confectioners' glue)*
- HERSHEY'S KISSESBRAND Chocolates or HUGSBRAND Candies, in pink and red foils
- Floralwire
- Clear cellophane or plastic wrap
- Florist tape
- Artificial leaves (optional)
- Ribbon

Use hot melt glue with adult supervision. Safe confectioners' glue recipe follows.

INSTRUCTIONS:

1. For each candy rose, spread confectioners' glue on bottom of one foil-wrapped chocolate. Firmly press the bottom of another chocolate to it.

2. Insert floral wire into one pointed end of double chocolate. Wrap 4-inch square of clear cellophane around double chocolate, twisting cellophane tightly around chocolate.

3. Starting at bottom of rose, wrap florist tape around edges of cellophane, continuing down the full length of wire with tape. Add 1 or 2 artificial leaves, if desired, securing leaves in place with florist tape.

4. Tie 2 or more candy roses together with a bow.

Note: Completed craft is for decorative purpose only. Candy should not be eaten.

Safe confectioners' glue: Gently stir together 4 teaspoons pasteurized dried egg whites (meringue powder) and ¼ cup warm water until completely dissolved. Beat in 3 cups sifted powdered sugar until thick and smooth. Use immediately. Cover with wet paper towel to keep from drying out.

Tip: You can make these into a bouquet or set in a vase for display.

creative crafts

KISSES® Acorn Treats

MATERIALS:

- **ROYAL ICING (recipe follows) or decorator's frosting**
- **HERSHEY'S KISSES**BRAND **Milk Chocolates**
- **Mini vanilla wafer cookies**
- **REESE'S Peanut Butter Chips or HERSHEY'S Butterscotch Chips**

INSTRUCTIONS:

1. Prepare ROYAL ICING and place in pastry bag with small tip. Remove wrappers from milk chocolates.

2. Place mini vanilla wafer cookies on tray or plate with flat side of cookie towards the top. Squeeze small amount of icing onto bottom of milk chocolate piece. Immediately press chocolate bottom onto vanilla wafer cookie. Allow icing to set.

3. Place small dab of icing on bottom of peanut butter chip or butterscotch chip; immediately attach to top of cookie to finish acorn.

Royal Icing: Stir together 1 cup plus 2 tablespoons powdered sugar, 1 tablespoon warm water and 1½ teaspoons pasteurized dried egg whites (meringue powder). Beat at medium speed of electric mixer until spreadable. Add additional water, 1 teaspoon at a time, to get desired consistency. Transfer icing to pastry bag with desired tip. Cover icing and tip of pastry bag with damp paper towel to keep icing from drying out. Makes about ½ cup icing.

Candy Bowl Centerpiece

MATERIALS:

- ROYAL ICING (recipe follows) or low temperature glue gun and glue sticks
- KIT KAT Bars
- Straight-sided glass bowl
- Ribbon
- Scissors
- REESE'S PIECES Candies or other assorted HERSHEY'S Candies

INSTRUCTIONS:

1. Prepare ROYAL ICING, if using. Cut bars into sticks along natural breaking points.

2. Place several drops of icing "glue" along back of each stick and immediately place against outside of bowl. Hold several minutes until icing starts to set and candy piece stays in position. Continue "gluing" sticks to outside of bowl until outside of bowl is covered. Allow icing glue to harden.

3. Tie ribbon around bowl and fill with REESE'S PIECES or other HERSHEY'S Candies.

Royal Icing: Stir together 2¼ cups powdered sugar, 2 tablespoons warm water and 1 tablespoon pasteurized dried egg whites (meringue powder). Beat at medium speed of electric mixer until spreadable. Add additional water, 1 teaspoon at a time, to get desired consistency. Transfer icing to pastry bag with small tip. Cover any remaining icing and tip of pastry bag with damp paper towels to keep icing from drying out. Makes about 1 cup icing.

creative crafts

Small KISSES® Christmas Tree

MATERIALS FOR ONE TREE:

- Ice cream sugar cone
- Aluminum foil
- Glue (low-temperature glue gun and glue sticks, non-toxic craft glue, glue stick or safe confectioners' glue)*
- 26 to 30 HERSHEY'S KISSESBRAND Chocolates in holiday foil
- ⅓ yard (¼-inch-wide) ribbon (optional)

*Use hot melt glue with adult supervision. Safe confectioners' glue recipe on page 112.

INSTRUCTIONS:

Cover each cone with aluminum foil, securing with glue. Push remaining foil inside open end of cone to add strength. Glue chocolates onto cone with the flat end of the chocolate on the foil surface. Begin around the base and work up to the top, alternating colors. Finish by adding a small bow to the top, if desired.

Finished Size: 5 inches high.

Note: Completed craft is for decorative purpose only. Candy should not be eaten.

creative crafts

HERSHEY'S® KISSES® Mice

MATERIALS:

- ¼ yard (½-inch-wide) pink grosgrain ribbon
- Scissors
- Glue (low-temperature glue gun and glue sticks, non-toxic craft glue, glue stick or safe confectioners' glue)*
- 4 HERSHEY'S KISSES BRAND Chocolates per pair of mice
- 1 sheet pink felt
- 4 jiggly eyes

*Use hot melt glue with adult supervision. Safe confectioners' glue recipe on page 112.

INSTRUCTIONS:

1. Create tails by cutting 2-inch lengths of pink grosgrain ribbons, pinch one end of the ribbon in half and glue to point of 1 chocolate.

2. Cut the ears out of the pink felt and glue the base of the heart shape to the top of the flat side of 1 chocolate, leaving the two curved shapes extending over the edge to form the ears.

3. Glue both chocolates together flat end to flat end with felt ears nesting in between.

4. Complete by gluing on the jiggly eyes.

Note: Completed craft is for decorative purpose only. Candy should not be eaten.

creative crafts

HUGS® & KISSES® Candy Box

MATERIALS:

72	to 74 HERSHEY'S KISSESʙʀᴀɴᴅ **Milk Chocolates, divided**
2	**tablespoons shortening (do not use butter, margarine, spread or oil)**
10	**HERSHEY'S HUGSʙʀᴀɴᴅ Candies, unwrapped**
11	**HERSHEY'S MINIATURES Chocolate Bars, unwrapped**
	HERSHEY'S BLISS Milk Chocolates

INSTRUCTIONS:

1. Trace 2 (6½-inch) heart shapes on paper; place on baking sheet. Top with wax paper.

2. Remove wrappers from KISSES Milk Chocolates, reserving 10 chocolates for decoration. Place remaining chocolate pieces and shortening in medium microwave-safe bowl. Microwave at MEDIUM (50%) 1 minute; stir. If necessary, microwave at MEDIUM an additional 15 seconds at a time, stirring after each heating, until chocolate is melted and smooth when stirred.

3. Set aside ¼ cup melted chocolate. Spread half of remaining chocolate on wax paper over each heart shape. Refrigerate until firm.

4. For candy box top, dip bottom of reserved KISSES Chocolates and HUGS Candies in remaining melted chocolate and alternately press in place along edge of heart. For candy box bottom, dip long edge and sides of small chocolate bars in melted chocolate. Press along edge of heart (see photo). Cut 1 chocolate bar in half for top of heart. Refrigerate until firm.

5. Fill candy box with truffles. Store in cool place or refrigerate.

creative crafts

HERSHEY'S® KISSES® Snowflake

MATERIALS:

- Pencil
- White poster board (about 3- to 4-inch square)
- Plastic cup or drinking glass
- Decorative-edged scissors designed for children
- 4 paint stirring sticks (available at paint stores)
- Glue (low-temperature glue gun and glue sticks, non-toxic craft glue, glue stick or safe confectioners' glue)*
- Silver metallic acrylic craft paint (or color of choice)
- ½-inch paint brush
- 6-inch length of ribbon (½-inch wide)
- 1 thumbtack
- About 14 HERSHEY'S KISSESBRAND Chocolates wrapped in holiday foil
- 4 silver and white glitter pipe cleaners
- Silver glitter glue

*Use hot melt glue with adult supervision. Safe confectioners' glue recipe on page 112.

INSTRUCTIONS:

1. Trace a 3-inch circle onto the poster board using the bottom of a plastic cup or glass as a template. Cut out the circle using the decorative-edged scissors.

2. Place a generous amount of glue in the center of each paint stick. To make the snowflake shape: first glue 2 sticks together in the center to form a cross shape. Add the next 2 sticks, overlapping them so that the result looks like eight evenly-spaced spokes on a wheel.

3. Paint both sides of the snowflake using the metallic paint. Let dry about 1 hour.

4. Place and glue the poster board circle on top. Let dry for a few hours.

5. Fold the ribbon in half and, with the thumbtack, attach it to the underside of the top of one of the paint sticks to create a loop for hanging.

6. Glue 1 chocolate on the end of each paint stick and glue 5 to 6 chocolates in the circle (one in the center and five around it), or glue them onto the sticks as desired.

7. Cut each pipe cleaner in half, and bend each to form a V-shape and glue one on each stick, about an inch or two below the chocolates.

Note: Completed craft is for decorative purpose only. Candy should not be eaten.

Spring Birdhouse Centerpiece

MATERIALS:

- 1 Styrofoam sheet (1×12×36 inches)
- Pencil
- Scissors
- 1 square of green felt, 2 of blue felt and 1 of yellow felt
- Glue (low-temperature glue gun and glue sticks, non-toxic craft glue, glue stick or safe confectioners' glue)*
- 5 wooden skewers
- Toothpicks
- 4 bags (10 to 11 ounces each) HERSHEY'S KISSESBRAND Chocolates in spring colors
- Floral wire
- Feather butterfly wings
- Spanish moss
- Small bird

*Use hot melt glue with adult supervision. Safe confectioners' glue recipe on page 112.

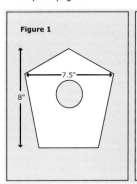

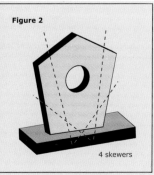

INSTRUCTIONS:

1. From a Styrofoam sheet, cut the 4 pieces of the birdhouse. Cut 1 (9×4-inch) piece to form the base, cut 2 (6×2-inch) pieces for the roof, then cut the front and back of the house using pattern provided (Figure 1).

2. Cover the base with green felt. Cut out 2 pieces from the blue felt to cover the Styrofoam of the front and back of the house. (Remember to cut out the hole in the center of both pieces.)

3. To assemble, place house in the center of the base, secure in place by using glue and 4 wooden skewers. Secure by inserting each skewer through the top of the house down through the base (Figure 2).

4. Attach the roof pieces using glue and securing with toothpicks. Cover both sides with yellow felt.

5. Decorate the birdhouse from the base up by gluing the flat end of the chocolates, spring colors, to the flat surface of the house. (Remember to decorate both sides if you plan to use as a table centerpiece.)

6. To make the springy buds in the garden, cut 5-inch lengths of floral wire and twirl each piece around a pencil to form the spring. Insert one end of wire into bottom of a pink KISSES Chocolate and the other end into the green base.

creative crafts

7. To make the butterfly, glue 2 chocolates' flat ends together with the feather wings between the chocolates. Using the same instructions as the springy buds, take a coiled wire and insert one end into the chocolate and the other end into the roof.

8. Complete by creating a nest out of Spanish moss for our bird to sit on. Insert a wooden skewer cut to 3-inch length through the house below the bird's nest for a perch.

Finished Size: 10 inches high×9 inches wide.

Note: Completed craft is for decorative purpose only. Candy should not be eaten.

HERSHEY'S® HUGS® & KISSES®
Chocolate Cards

MATERIALS:

- Store-bought cards
- Construction paper, scrapbook papers
- Scraps of ribbon, trims, embellishments, etc.
- Glue (low-temperature glue gun and glue sticks, non-toxic craft glue, glue stick or safe confectioners' glue)*
- HERSHEY'S KISSESBRAND Milk Chocolates and HERSHEY'S HUGSBRAND Candies

*Use hot melt glue with adult supervision. Safe confectioners' glue recipe on page 112.

INSTRUCTIONS:

Create sweet and original cards to carry your wishes. Decorate a homemade card, a computer-generated card or even a store-bought card with HUGS Candies or KISSES Chocolates and make your message even more personal. Use some of our ideas in the picture or create your own.

Note: Completed craft is for decorative purpose only. Candy should not be eaten.

creative crafts

HERSHEY'S® KISSES® Kritters

MATERIALS:

- Glue (low-temperature glue gun and glue sticks, non-toxic craft glue, glue stick or safe confectioners' glue)*
- Butterfly wings/feathers (available at craft stores or make your own)
- 2 HERSHEY'S KISSESBRAND Chocolates per Kritter
- Pipe cleaners
- Construction paper, felt or foam sheets
- Jiggly eyes

*Use hot melt glue with adult supervision. Safe confectioners' glue recipe on page 112.

INSTRUCTIONS:

KISSES Butterfly

1. Glue 1 pair of butterfly wings to the flat side of 1 chocolate.

2. Bend a 2-inch piece of pipe cleaner in half and curl both ends.

3. Glue folded point to top end of same chocolate.

4. Glue second chocolate flat end to flat end with other chocolate, securing the wings and antennae between them.

5. Complete by gluing on jiggly eyes.

KISSES Katerpillar

1. Curl a 6-inch piece of pipe cleaner around a pencil. Glue 1 chocolate to each end of the curled pipe cleaner.

2. Fold a 1-inch piece of pipe cleaner in half and glue to top of 1 chocolate to form antennae.

3. Cut 2 sets of feet. Glue to bottom of each chocolate.

4. Complete by gluing on jiggly eyes.

KISSES Ostrich

1. Bend pipe cleaner in half.

2. Glue the center of the bent pipe cleaner to an edge of the flat side of 1 chocolate.

3. Glue feather to the opposite edge of the flat side of the same chocolate.

4. Glue second chocolate flat end to flat end with other chocolate, securing the feather and pipe cleaner in between them.

5. Complete by gluing on jiggly eyes to 1 chocolate and feathers to the sides of the other chocolate.

Note: Completed craft is for decorative purpose only. Candy should not be eaten.

Star of David Ornament

3. Glue a chocolate to each tip of star.

4. Add thread at one end to hang in home.

Note: Completed craft is for decorative purpose only. Candy should not be eaten.

MATERIALS:

- **6 craft sticks**
- **Glitter**
- **Glue (low-temperature glue gun and glue sticks, non-toxic craft glue, glue stick or safe confectioners' glue)***
- **6 HERSHEY'S KISSES**BRAND **Chocolates filled with Caramel**
- **Embroidery thread**

*Use hot melt glue with adult supervision. Safe confectioners' glue recipe on page 112.

INSTRUCTIONS:

1. Make Star of David shapes from craft sticks. Glue together.

2. Add glitter on each star.

creative crafts

index

METRIC CONVERSION CHART

VOLUME MEASUREMENTS (dry)

1/8 teaspoon = 0.5 mL
1/4 teaspoon = 1 mL
1/2 teaspoon = 2 mL
3/4 teaspoon = 4 mL
1 teaspoon = 5 mL
1 tablespoon = 15 mL
2 tablespoons = 30 mL
1/4 cup = 60 mL
1/3 cup = 75 mL
1/2 cup = 125 mL
2/3 cup = 150 mL
3/4 cup = 175 mL
1 cup = 250 mL
2 cups = 1 pint = 500 mL
3 cups = 750 mL
4 cups = 1 quart = 1 L

VOLUME MEASUREMENTS (fluid)

1 fluid ounce (2 tablespoons) = 30 mL
4 fluid ounces (1/2 cup) = 125 mL
8 fluid ounces (1 cup) = 250 mL
12 fluid ounces (1 1/2 cups) = 375 mL
16 fluid ounces (2 cups) = 500 mL

WEIGHTS (mass)

1/2 ounce = 15 g
1 ounce = 30 g
3 ounces = 90 g
4 ounces = 120 g
8 ounces = 225 g
10 ounces = 285 g
12 ounces = 360 g
16 ounces = 1 pound = 450 g

DIMENSIONS

1/16 inch = 2 mm
1/8 inch = 3 mm
1/4 inch = 6 mm
1/2 inch = 1.5 cm
3/4 inch = 2 cm
1 inch = 2.5 cm

OVEN TEMPERATURES

250°F = 120°C
275°F = 140°C
300°F = 150°C
325°F = 160°C
350°F = 180°C
375°F = 190°C
400°F = 200°C
425°F = 220°C
450°F = 230°C

BAKING PAN SIZES

Utensil	Size in Inches/Quarts	Metric Volume	Size in Centimeters
Baking or Cake Pan (square or rectangular)	8×8×2	2 L	20×20×5
	9×9×2	2.5 L	23×23×5
	12×8×2	3 L	30×20×5
	13×9×2	3.5 L	33×23×5
Loaf Pan	8×4×3	1.5 L	20×10×7
	9×5×3	2 L	23×13×7
Round Layer Cake Pan	8×1½	1.2 L	20×4
	9×1½	1.5 L	23×4
Pie Plate	8×1¼	750 mL	20×3
	9×1¼	1 L	23×3
Baking Dish or Casserole	1 quart	1 L	—
	1½ quarts	1.5 L	—
	2 quarts	2 L	—